ORDEAL BY INNOCENCE

by

Marguerite Wellbourne

Copyright © 2018 by Maureen Larter.
First published 2018. Sweetfields Publishing
Cover design by Francessca Wingfield - UK
956 Comboyne Rd, Cedar Party, NSW Australia 2429
email: maureenlarter@gmail.com
blog :- readeatdream.net
twitter:- @maureenlarter
facebook:- www.facebook.com/EbooksbyMaureenLarter
Author pages: viewAuthor.at/MaureenLarter
viewAuthor.at/Marguerite Wellbourne

A catalogue record for this book is available from
The National Library of Australia, Canberra, ACT, Australia

Set in Times New Roman font by
Maureen Larter, Cedar Party, NSW, Australia.

Other books written by Maureen Larter

Good Health – The Soil

Gardening Guides
- Summer
- Autumn
- Winter
- Spring
- Yearly flowers and vegetable guide

Adult Drama
(under the pen-name Marguerite Wellbourne)

Tarnished Gems
Ordeal by Innocence

Business (How to) Booklet

The Start of Something Big

Short Stories

- Book 1 - At the Beach - (4 stories)
- Book 2 – Predicaments – (5 stories)

Books for young girls

Fairies from Aurora Village Series
1. Broken Wing.
2. Spiders, Lizards and Flies
3. Cave of the Golden Bower Bird

Novels for Middle School Children

- In Search of the Elusive Panda (A Kathy Edwards Adventure)
- Petey - Missing the Migration

For Toddlers

Alphabet Animals of Australia Series

- Angus Ant and the Acrobats
- Betty Bee's Birthday Bash
- Ben Brolga's Band
- Candy Cow and the Caterpillar
- Cassie Crocodile Catches a Cold
- Dorothy Dog and the Dangerous Dragonfly.
- Evie Emu's Encounter
- Frank Frog Feels Foolish
- Giddy the Galah
- Helen Heron and the Helicopter
- Iggy Ibis is Important
- John Jabiru and the Jolly Jam tin
- Kathy Koala's Kerfuffle
- Larry Lyrebird Laughs

This is an ongoing series. There are many more to come.

More picture books
- Arabella's Tree
- What about me

Check out readeatdream.net for more up to date lists.

Ordeal by Innocence.

Chapter 1.

The image flashed into my mind. I would close my eyes and wish it away - but it kept returning. It was always there. I knew it would never go away.

At first I hadn't thought it would mean so much. That it wouldn't always haunt me. I thought I was strong. But the image stayed and with it came the fear.

I remembered crawling along, moving slowly and tortuously. The tears had been running down my cheeks and blood trailed behind me as the vestiges of the horror kept draining from me. When I finally collapsed, the mental pain overcame the rest. I felt as if I lay on the carpet for hours. The hallway looked as if it was miles long every time my eyes flickered open and I wished I could move. The carpet felt harsh and scratchy, and the walls seemed to close in. When I tried to get up, all I could feel was the pain. I lay, not daring to even try to crawl, as everything became too much to bear.

I was alone

I had never been so alone.

My soul screeched silently inside my head so full of the grief.

Just as I sank into a strange oblivion, I was jerked back. There was no escape. The image flashed before me keeping me from peace – that blood soaked picture in my brain.

Why? Why did it happen to me?

I didn't understand. This wasn't meant to be.

The sound of whimpering assaulted my ears. When I realised it was me, it took all my courage and concentration to stop. When silence returned, it was no better.

Thoughts kept pounding at me.

This is all my own fault.

No-one will show love, or compassion. There will be people turn away from me, pretend it hadn't happened, not willing to talk and help.

What could I say to my husband now?

What would my parents think of me?

In the depths of my heart, hope had shrivelled. The future seemed bleak. The fear trembled within me.

What if it never got any better?

What if this was my last chance?

Somehow I rallied. I dragged myself to the bedroom and clawed my way onto the haven and softness of my bed. As I sank onto the bed I wondered whether I would make it through the afternoon.

I felt cold.

I felt violated.

I couldn't get warm.

There was emptiness and there was pain.

Twice I crept out of the bedroom and changed my blood soaked clothes – but it didn't take away the pain. In the bathroom, trying to clean myself, I noticed my reflection in the mirror. My face was stark, shocked and gaunt. My eyes looked hollow, red and swollen, aching from the constant tears. I stared down at the blood. The stain was so fresh, the metallic smell over-powering.

This hadn't happened, surely. This happened to other people, weaker people, unlucky people. Not to me!

Slowly the day wore on.

I stayed alone and afraid, too tired and sore to venture far.

What would happen now?

How could I go on?

I heard the clock strike three. He would be home soon.

I had to get up. Be clean. Smiling. Putting on my brave face. He mustn't know. He will be so angry.

I staggered from the bed, feeling washed out and exhausted.

And there it was again.

I stood, frozen, swaying with renewed pain, the blood still oozing.

That image! The dreadful picture seared into the space behind my eyes. Something I would never lose. Something that wrung a wailing groan of anguish from my body as I stood there.

My dead baby floating in the bowl. Such a tiny shred of flesh, covered in blood and wrapped in translucent skin. The rejection, by my body, of a living soul.

My dream of motherhood gone. Even worse than all the other hurts I had sustained by his hand.

How had it come to this?

Chapter 2.

School was a wondrous place. I loved it.

OK - so I was a little strange.

I loved the learning, the books and the company. But it had always been a struggle, too. Trying to have friends was the hardest part of the equation. Throughout the years, teachers watched me stumble through the process of friendship. I preferred the silence of solitude. I enjoyed the process of educating myself. I spent hours gaining knowledge and reading novels.

No wonder other children never got too close to me. I never realised that so many of my class mates didn't like school, were annoyed that they had to sit and listen to boring teachers spouting work for them to do. I sat transfixed by the teachers - little gods in my opinion - especially as the years passed and I advanced to the latter part of my schooling.

Mind you, as I grew older, I would listen to those around me and it always amazed me. The girls sighed and drooled over the boys. The boys ogled and strutted around the girls.

Me?

I sat under the trees, ignoring the weird social behaviour going on around me. I concentrated - my head down reading the book open on my lap!

And if I wasn't in the mood to read, I'd be looking at the grass and the insects scurrying around, or at the weed flowers, so beautiful and yet so unappreciated. Nature was so wonderful that it took my breath away.

I was looked upon by the others in my class as something a little odd, someone who didn't fit in. These days I would be called a bit of a nerd.

A geek.

It didn't help that I was neither pretty nor well proportioned. Or the fact that I wore glasses and became the 'teacher's pet'.

It was a lonely time, yet I wasn't lonely. A conundrum, if ever there was one. Deep down I knew I wasn't popular and I would have liked to be. But, somehow, I divorced myself from the feeling and tried to embrace my solitude.

***

It wasn't until my parents moved and I had to change schools that life changed for me forever.

Right from the first day at my new school I made a decision. No more would I be teacher's pet. No more would I disappear into the background. No more the 'good' girl for me.

I'd had years of a starry-eyed awe of learning and I had listened to teachers with rapt attention. In consequence, I had put myself above the other kids in my class, and they kept their distance. I had sailed through my childhood with no friends.

I hadn't realised that friendship depended on a shared rebellion of the traditions of education. Teachers were not to be liked, homework was not to be completed, and learning was only to be tolerated for as long as it may be of use. After all, what use was algebra, knowing the history of the Anglo-Saxon race, studying World War One and Two? It all seemed to be a useless exercise that was forced upon the young.

Well, that was the prevailing view of teenagers. I was going to fit in even if it went against my true feelings.

So....

I put a swagger in my steps and a loud mouth into my persona. Nobody in my new school would ever notice a hint of my love of learning.

Of course, it wasn't quite as easy as I had imagined. The tests came and went, and I passed them all with flying colours. I couldn't stop myself from joining the choir, the drama group - and horror of horrors, even the chess club!

But the one truly great part of my transformation was that I met my best friend, Amy.

She was, in my eyes, the most wonderful friend to have. I was in awe! She was gorgeous to look at, with a figure to die for. Everyone in the class liked her. As I got to know her, I discovered that, behind the rebellious and outspoken popular girl, was a shy, serious, studious person trying to hide away - just like me.

I couldn't believe she had decided I was worth being her friend, so I clung to her as if my life had just begun and she was the only thing keeping me from disappearing. We went everywhere together. We spoke back to the teachers, we refused to wear a school uniform and we drooled over the 'bad' boys in the next year, those that would be leaving the school at the end of the year.

We envied their luck. Amy became even more outspoken and a flouter of rules. She became more and more boy crazy and flirtatious. Her serious and studious side became buried and forgotten. Well, at least it seemed to. I played along, making it sound as if I was experienced and worldly, just like her. It was a good act, but I knew I was lying.

And to top it all off, I really liked one particular boy.

Looking back on it now, I realize it was probably the worst idea I'd ever had.

Daz was the worst offender in the school. He wore a leather jacket, rode a motorcycle and smoked behind closed doors. If you can imagine the *'Fonz'* of *'Happy Days'* and *'Danny'* from *'Grease'* all rolled into one - that was Daz! He was the ultimate *'Rebel without a cause'*. His brown hair was slicked back into a coif Elvis would have been proud of. He was tall and yet well built, his jeans moulding to his behind like a rubber glove fits a hand! His eyes were a startling and penetrating blue when he looked at you. He would saunter into a room and the magnetism exuded from him so strongly, most people stopped what they were doing and stared.

In my eyes, he was my hero. I couldn't believe he had the courage to act the way he did.

Silently I worshipped him - the old cliché - a crush so bad that I must have worn the look of obvious adoration on my face as I made sure I was always within sight of him. I trailed around after him like a fool.

Amy tutted

"Oh God, Clare!" She hit me lightly on the arm as she rolled her eyes. "Give me a break! You're doing it again!"

"What?"

"Ah, come on, girl - you're away with the Daz fairies, aren't you?"

"How...?"

"It's written all over your face! Anyways, forget Daz - he's no good for you. Not like Billy - if only *he'd* look at me!!" She moaned, clasping her hands over her heart and closing her eyes in a semblance of a romantic swoon. So... today it was Billy! That was doomed to failure. Inwardly I groaned. He was a creep; a criminal in the making, if I was any judge.

Typical.

She couldn't help herself – she had a weakness for the 'bad boys' in school.

"Weren't you going out with Ian?" I frowned

"Oh him? Nah. Not anymore. He's a creep!"

I shook my head and went back to thinking about Daz while she went back to sneaking sideways glances at Billy as he swaggered over to a group of boys at the edge of the oval.

When Daz finally noticed me, it was for the strangest reason.

I'd had enough of wishing my life away and I decided to turn my attention to playing hockey.

It was a fad at the school at the time. Every lunch time groups formed themselves into teams and raced around playing a truncated game of no-rules hockey. For the first couple of days I sat on the sidelines and watched.

That's when it happened.

The hockey ball, hard and dirty white, blurred in its flight towards me.

I stared.

I blinked.

I couldn't move.

Wham!

Straight into my knee! It was as if I'd been hit by a long-range missile. And it was horrific.

I went down like a ton of potatoes, writhing in agony, my knee already swollen and going a peculiar shade of blue.

When a hand reached out and took mine, I couldn't see who it was through the tears but you will have already figured that out, haven't you?

"You OK?" asked Daz.

I didn't know what to say, even if I could have answered, so I nodded. Tears of pain and humiliation threatened to fall. My eyes watered and I bit my lip as I tried to smile. No way was I going to show him that I was a wimp, but I was a mess inside. My heart beat so loudly you would think it would have burst.

Somehow, I got back to the classroom, and gratefully sat at my desk for the rest of the afternoon. Daz surprised me by making a point of seeing me later to check and see if I was able to get home. He offered, and I accepted, a ride home on his motorbike.

I was hooked.

It seems weird now that that was the start of our unlikely friendship.

Of course, it didn't go terribly well at the beginning. He teased me and mocked me, causing me to blush and stammer whenever he was near.

He thought it was amusing, but I was over the moon inside my mortification.

Why?

Because I coveted every conversation, taking out each word and studying it as if my life depended on it.

I continued to worship and he continued to mock. There was no dating, no hand-holding, no progress, yet we were aware of each other and at times of hardship or when others were rude to me, he became my shield, my sanctuary.

This fragile friendship lasted for the rest of my schooling.

***

Amy continued to fall in and out of love with one male after another. After we left school, she began an apprenticeship at the local hairdressers. We stayed close friends, and, although I had gone on to University, we met every chance we could.

One Sunday over a cup of coffee at the local café, she confessed to me in exasperation.

"I'm so over men!" she said, running her fingers through her newly permed golden locks as she grimaced. "They're only after one thing, you know."

I frowned at her.

"Oh, come on!" I smiled. "You over men? I don't believe you!"

She grinned back at me.

"Yeah. Well! I've been lookin' for Mr. Right for ages." she took a breath and giggled.

"Guess I haven't been lookin' real careful tho' 'cos I don't reckon he's out there! The blokes I've met are all tarred with the same brush. Gawd! I'm sick of fighting them off with a stick!"

"I wish!" I sighed as I thought about Daz. "I've not even been kissed yet!"

"Really?" Amy looked at me with mock horror. "Well, lucky you. All this talk about sex and boys - it's not all it's cracked up to be."

There were several conversations like that over the months of my first year at Uni. It seemed to happen every time Amy broke up with her current flame. It never took her long to find the next handsome hunk and our friendship suffered her extreme highs and then corresponding lows while I buried myself in study.

Around the end of my first year of my degree, she rang me on a Friday and asked if I would meet her at 'our' café in the main street.

I dashed down from Uni to meet her. It was unusual to meet on a week day - we made a point of always meeting on the weekends. I knew something needed to be discussed; there was obviously something wrong.

When I saw her sitting at the table over by the window, I took a few moments to watch her. She was staring, unseeing, out of the window, her chin in her hand, her thin elbow leaning on the faded green tabletop. I thought she looked as if she may have been crying. I'd never seen her so depressed before and it surprised me.

The seats in the café were hard wooden benches with laminex-topped tables in rows the depth of the room. I slid in to the seat opposite her, wishing there was a more comfortable spot. She didn't move, didn't acknowledge that she was aware of my presence so I waited, not making a sound. To fill the awkward silence until she was ready to talk, I looked at the wall on the other side of the room. Faces of smiling pop stars stared down at us from black frames on dirty khaki walls. Amy still hadn't moved.

The smiling faces on the wall didn't really register and I couldn't wait any longer. My patience snapped.

"What's happened?"

Her shoulders slumped and she turned a vacant face in my direction. She didn't speak. The words seemed to be straining to escape, but her lips tightened.

"Amy! This isn't like you!" I tried again. "Tell me!"

"Don't worry!" She sighed, then turned once more to look out of the window. Her hazel eyes seemed clouded and troubled, and I doubted if she saw the scene on the other side of the glass. I waited again. I couldn't push her into telling me anything if she wasn't happy to confide.

"I'm just a bit depressed, today." she murmured, talking to the window in such a low voice I wondered if she had actually spoken. I strained towards her.

"Pardon?"

She still continued to stare into nothingness.

I took a sip of the coffee that the waitress had plonked down in front of us several minutes before. A drip slipped off the bottom of the mug and landed on my new t-shirt. I grimaced, but left it alone. I could see Amy wanted to tell me something, but didn't know where to start.

She took a deep breath, and blew it out as if the tension could disappear with the expelled air.

She turned.

Grabbing her bag, she took an old photo and a letter out of one of the pockets and thrust it across the table in front of me. Tears filled her eyes and she sniffed, wiping at her nose with the back of her hand.

She took another deep breath as my hand hovered over the two well-fingered crinkled envelope and a photo on the table.

She spoke, her voice cracking with the emotion. I almost got out of the chair to hug her, but what she said left me as shocked as she was.

"She's been lying to me," she sniffed again, bending her head to search in the depths of her handbag for a handkerchief. She pulled out a wrinkled well used piece of cloth and wiped her nose. Her eyes were moist as she looked at me with a stunned expression, the tears held back by pure pride.

I hadn't moved, nor did I dare. I felt that if I did or said anything she would withdraw and become the girl I knew from school days - a smiling face, hiding the grief.

I waited.

"Open it!" She pointed at the envelope on the table. "I can't look at it! I tried, but I just couldn't get passed the first few words!"

I didn't know what to do. I picked up the photo instead and idly turned it over. On the back it had a date, then two names. One was Amy's mother; the other was a man's name - someone I had never heard of before. The next words made my eyebrows lift in surprise. It said 'Honeymoon, Greece'.

I looked up at my friend. She was staring at the table as if it was a priceless painting. She placed her hands on the table, her fingers nervously tracing the patterns in the laminex. She didn't stop watching her hand, but spoke in a gritty, determined voice.

"Please. Open the letter - I can't bear to do it again!"

I carefully picked up the envelope. It wasn't sealed.

"Have you read it?" I asked. "It's been opened."

"I told you - I tried. I just couldn't get the courage up to continue - not after I read the first couple of sentences," she replied. "Mum left it on the hall cupboard when she left for work this morning."

I slid the letter from the envelope and unfolded the paper.

'My darling daughter,' I read.

'This may come as a bit of a shock, but I need to tell you I will not be coming home anymore. I love you dearly, but my marriage to Chas has broken down. I also need to tell you that Chas took me in when I was pregnant with you. He is not your father, although he has loved you as his daughter. Your father was my first husband, and he died during a storm while out on his fishing boat. I discovered I was pregnant while I was fighting a grief that no one has the right to suffer. I didn't want you at the time, but Chas came into my life and made me fight for the life I

had and the life of my baby. When you were born, I was so glad I had kept you and I married Chas, more out of obligation than love. It is amazing that our marriage has worked as well as it has, as over the years all I could think of was the love that I had lost, when your father never came back from his fishing trip.

Please forgive me for being a coward and leaving this letter for you to read, rather than having the courage to face you and Chas with this truth. I needed to get out so that I can try and fix the mistakes I've made and mend what I consider to be my broken life, without anyone pulling me this way and that and manipulating my heart.

As soon as I find a place to live and manage to get my life back, I will let you know where I am.

Please remember - I love you.

Your Mum. xxxx'

I hadn't realized I had read the words aloud, but when I looked up, Amy's face was chalky white, tears trickling down her cheeks; her eyes had lost the light of life. And yet, there wasn't a shred of compassion in them.

It took several minutes of stunned silence, then the sounds of the traffic outside and the low mumble of the customers inside slowly filtered into the bubble of disbelief that seemed to envelop us. A baby cried, a car tooted, a magpie chortled. Outside, as I, in my turn, stared unseeing through the window, a woman rushed past with bags of goodies clasped in her hands, a couple of teenagers sauntered along, laughing and giggling.

Life was still going on.

Other people were acting normally and yet in that small cubicle in a shabby café, everything had changed. I forced myself to turn and look at Amy.

"I'm so sorry." I managed to squeeze out. I guess I was as shocked as her. Chas and Monica had seemed such a perfect couple. It shows how no-one should take face values as true.

We both stared out of the window now, not knowing what to say to each other. Our half-drunk coffees were cold and forgotten. A young, handsome man drove up to the café on a bicycle. He parked his bike, and turned and gave us a smile.

To my surprise I saw Amy smile back.

"Well!" she said, once more wiping her face with a quick flash of her handkerchief. "You'd better order another coffee - this one's cold."

I frowned, but Amy turned towards the door and grinned at the young man as he entered the café. It seemed that she was going to pretend the letter never existed, that the news it contained was no more important than the coffee drip stain on my t-shirt that was now a distant memory.

I stood up. "Are you alright?" I asked.

She stared at me somewhat vacantly. "Mmmm?"

Then she turned away, ignoring me, once again putting on the face that I knew from school - the face that pushed away the emotions, the face that told the world she was okay, brilliantly happy, with nothing to worry about. I shook my head, knowing it was false, but got up and made my way to the counter to order another coffee. As I glanced over my shoulder to make sure she was okay, she had already begun checking out the young man. I felt like going back and giving her a good shake, telling her to cry, give in to the feelings churning inside of her, but I knew it was no good. She would be horrified that I would consider that she should show her pain, admit to the heartache, and show that she was soft and hurting.

Amy changed that day. Her behaviour became more and more bizarre. There was an iciness in her eyes and a hardness added to all she did. Her penchant for changing boyfriends became extreme. She took her hurt out on the males she met, and I couldn't do a darn thing to help her.

By the time I brought the cups of coffee back to the table, the young man was already sitting at our table, and Amy was talking animatedly to him.

She turned a glowing smile in my direction.

"Clare - this is Damien. I saw him outside and thought I knew him, but it turns out I was wrong!"

"Lovely to meet you."

I could feel the smile on my face, but it felt stiff and forced as inwardly I cringed. I knew Amy had only told a white lie; it was one of her favourite pick-up lines.

The next quarter of an hour was a nightmare for me. I wanted to talk, to make sure my friend was okay; to pursue the subject, see if I could find out what Amy would do. See if I could help in any way. But I wasn't given the chance.

The time trickled by, with Amy and Damien making small talk. I could see that there would be a date come from this for Amy.

I sat quietly, letting their conversation blur into the background, as my mind churned with thoughts.

After what I had just learnt, I knew I was fortunate. My parents were so happy together that I was almost an outsider in the family. Even so, my family was one of happiness, love and stability. I couldn't imagine how Amy must be feeling. The look, with the unshed tears and hardness in her eyes she had given me, had been strange. It needed explanation. Why would she be so cold within, yet have tears nearly falling at the same time? Had there always been tension in Amy's home? Was she hurting for her mother, the betrayal, or her own loss? I had no idea. I was ashamed to admit to myself that I knew very little about her life; that our friendship had always been shallow.

At the end of fifteen minutes, as I sipped my coffee distractedly, listening to the murmur of the conversation between Amy and the young man, she stood up, grasped Damien by the arm and tapped my shoulder with the other.

"Thanks, Clare." she said as she swept the photo and letter into her handbag, "I'll see you 'round."

She sashayed out of the café arm in arm with the young man whom she and I had only just met. I was left sitting, stunned, trying to work out what had just happened.

As I reflected on the momentous events in my friend's life, I came to the conclusion, once again, that I was so lucky. How Amy could have dismissed the shock of her mother's letter was beyond me. My parents, while not being completely perfect, were obviously in love with one another - almost to the point of obsession. I know that I often felt lonely and neglected, while they had eyes only for each other, but at least they were there. How I would cope if one of them left was something I didn't want to contemplate.

I sat and stared at my empty coffee cup, and Amy's full one. It was so cold the milk was like a dirty skin floating above a brown ocean. She hadn't even had time to drink before she was once again off with a man. Now I could see it for what it was - a vain attempt to cover up any chink of feeling - a case of 'use and abuse', so that she could wallow in her bad behaviour instead of facing the demons of truth. How would the hurt she was feeling manifest itself? What would she do next to bury her feelings even deeper? So much for her declaration that she was 'over men'!

Thank goodness I didn't have such an experience. I don't know what I would do if I did. My life was all peaches and cream compared to hers.

***

I walked away from the café in a daze. I couldn't focus on anything. It felt like I was under water, wallowing around, unable to breathe. If the other people in the street noticed, they certainly didn't show it.

Well, if they did, at least I wasn't aware.

Even if they had all stopped and stared at me with open mouths and incredulous faces, pointing wildly in my direction, I am sure I would still have been oblivious. All I could do was go over the events that had just taken place. My thoughts tumbled around and around, trying to put the whole ridiculous situation into some sort of order.

How could Amy just ignore such a letter? How could she feel nothing? Was she crying inside and covering it up with a facade of cheerfulness? To make matters worse, she had latched onto a stranger, and hadn't felt that I was a good enough friend to take the brunt of any emotions that might have surfaced.

It didn't make sense. She must be horrified on the inside, whatever her appearance suggested.

I certainly was.

I put a hand to the black velvet choker that I had worn to complement my new t-shirt (with the brand new coffee stain) and black skirt, almost ripping it off as if it was indeed strangling me.

I stopped in midstride and tried to focus my eyes.

I was standing in a park, near a bench seat. Two dogs gambolling around in front of me nearly knocked me off my feet, so I sat down with relief.

My thoughts became a mess of tangled threads. Life was so uncertain. What if something happened to my parents? What if something happened to me? What if the world collapsed? What if...? What if...?

I realized I was beginning to panic. Slowly but surely I forced myself to be rational, to settle. I took a deep breath and looked around. Gradually the world returned to normal.

Behind me, two children were laughing and giggling as they played with their dogs. A couple on my left, lounging on a picnic blanket, arms entwined, looked as if they were lost in a circle of rapt seclusion. The sun came out and spotlighted them in golden rays, as if the Universe was watching and approving. An elderly man shuffled along the pathway nearby, rugged up against his perception of coldness, lost in memories. Two young lads sat on a protruding platform over the lake, fishing rods dangling in the water. I suspected their bait had long since gone as they talked animatedly about some favourite topic or other of theirs, voices excited and raised with the fire of passion.

Without warning Daz's face swam into view behind my eyelids. He had never realized that I had been so in love with him. He had treated me like a favourite toy, but I had been so blinded by my feelings, I had no idea what he really had felt. Was he stringing me along? Or was the teasing and mocking a way to show that he liked me? Were we really friends or had I misread the whole relationship?

If Amy's situation had taught me anything, it was that life was short, so confusing, so much of a gamble. That in an instant, life can change, that there were so many variables that could go wrong, that other people's actions were not mine to control. The obvious conclusion was that I should face the possibilities and get what I want now. Letting life pass me by, waiting for someone out there in the world to come to me with my wants on a platter just wasn't going to happen.

So I decided as I sat on that bench watching the world of strangers, feeling the pain of Amy's mother's actions.

I would find Daz again.

I would let him know that I loved him.

I stood up - no longer worried and fragile. Amy's mother's letter and Amy's reaction had been my catalyst. University and my teaching course could wait. Mum and Dad would be disappointed, but I was no longer interested in long hours of study. I'd go back to it after I'd found Daz. I'd get an extension, an exemption for the rest of the year. Suddenly love was more important. The crush from high school had to be resolved.

Amy was going to have to face her own battles, I had mine to conquer and I was ready.

Life was going to get better from now on.

I re-adjusted the choker, brushed down my skirt, adjusted my t-shirt and stood up. I strode away from that park as if the fury of hell's monsters was following me. If they had attacked me, in my present mood I wouldn't have shortened my steps, merely turned and brushed them aside.

I was ready for whatever came my way. I felt no fear. A failed marriage, an emotionless friend, a daunting love affair, a careless truck driver, a fearsome enemy - they were nothing in the face of my determination to start living.

***

When I finally stopped walking, it was because my energy was spent. I had no idea where I was, and I felt completely drained. The sky had darkened, and it took me a few seconds to realise it was nightfall, not a storm. My feelings were still volatile and spun around inside me like a whirlpool, and I wouldn't have been the slightest surprised if the Power of the Universe had sent lightning and thunder in response, but when I looked, the sky was clear and the stars bright.

I stood on the sidewalk and tried to work out where I was.

Nothing looked familiar.

The night's darkness intensified, and lights began to illuminate the house windows around me. A cat yowled, a dog barked, someone in a nearby house turned up a radio and I heard the distinctive music that began the news broadcast... and then I heard footsteps.

My heart jumped, then began to race. I daren't turn. The bravery and determination, that only a few minutes ago had had me striding along like an angry impresario, evaporated in an instant. Who was behind me? The sound of the steps began to hurry, so I recommenced my journey at a firm and purposeful speed. Walking on to I knew not where. The footsteps behind me began to speed up, and so did I.

Suddenly a child ran around me, and I stopped as the young boy sped on, turning into a gate not far ahead. The front door opened and a woman's voice yelled at the boy, clipping him around the ears as they both disappeared from view.

The door slammed.

I tried to settle myself as I continued walking, my heart finally slowing its beat to a comfortable speed. I mentally shook myself.

I was a grown woman. My reaction had been extreme. I had lost the strength of the fury and passion that had begun my journey. I was wilting, energy all gone.

I could see a street junction coming up, and when I reached the corner, I looked both ways to try and get my bearings.

To the left I could see a few shops, so I turned and made my way towards them.

***

I stood in front of the fish and chip shop and gathered my thoughts while I controlled my breathing until it slowed and the flutters in my stomach calmed. It took me a moment or two to realise that I had walked non-stop all afternoon. My feet were aching and now that I had stopped I realized I was exhausted.

I walked into the shop, pushing aside the plastic fly barrier, the strips fluttering past my face. The smell of stale oil and cooked chips spilled onto the pavement behind me.

Was it really four hours since I had been sitting with Amy drinking tepid coffee? My feet were telling me that it was; the flat shoes I wore had not saved my heels from stinging blisters.

I groped around in my handbag and pulled out my purse. The woman behind the counter waited for my order, her eyes blank with boredom.

I tried to smile, but the woman continued to wait, her lips curled slightly in a line of disapproval.

"Can I have some chips?" I asked.

"Small or large?" The question was automatic and said flatly.

"Um. Er..." I blinked rapidly and tried to bring my brain back to the present.

"Small, please."

"Chicken salt or plain?"

I frowned.

"Plain will be fine," I swallowed, then licked my lips. I continued.

"Excuse me," I ventured a little nervously. "I wonder if you could tell me which suburb I'm in?"

The lady behind the counter grinned suddenly, her eyes widening.

"Had one too many, love?" she asked.

I realised how silly I must have sounded and I shook my head.

"No," I smiled back at her. "I've been walking for hours, thinking and thinking - wasn't taking too much notice of where I walked." I lifted my eyebrows and grimaced a little. "Silly of me, I suppose."

"Here, love," she grinned and handed me a glass of water and a plastic wrapped sandwich with the chips. "You must have had a bad morning then!"

I rummaged around in my purse, but before I could get out some money, she waved her hand.

"Put it away - I can see when someone needs a helping hand."

I was so grateful I burst into tears, and she hurried around the counter and came over to give me a hug. By the time I'd stopped sobbing and apologising, I'd found out I was about 5 kilometres from home. I sat and ate the soggy sandwich, drank the water and clutched the hot chips to my chest. The t-shirt sucked up an oil stain to join the coffee mark as I thanked the lady. It had restored some of my faith in the human race, and I refused her help to get home, even though my feet were now throbbing with pain.

I staggered outside and headed back the way I had come. If I saw a taxi I was going to give in and get a ride home.

I'd only gone about a kilometre when I felt the strangest feeling. The street was empty and the trees in the front yards of all the houses seemed to close in on me. I suddenly heard footsteps behind me.

Again.

I shook my head as if to clear any lingering cobwebs. This time I was not going to give in to any irrational fear, but then a taxi turned the corner and I waved it down with gratitude.

***

When I finally walked in to my flat, I breathed a sigh of relief. I flopped down on the comfortable but well-worn sofa and kicked off my shoes. My heels were rubbed raw. It was 9.30pm. Where had the time gone?

I yawned. The day had been one of the worst I had had in a long time. I sometimes wished, when these types of days occurred, that I was still living at home.

But I wasn't.

I had struck out on my own when I'd started Uni, and was proud of my little one bedroom flat. The rent was minimal, but that was my only concession to my parents - they paid it.

The furnishings were still very basic, and the rooms small, but cosy. My sofa was one of the first pieces of furniture I had bought. It was a dull brown, but the cushions were thick and soft. I could easily have curled up and slept right where I sat, but I needed a cup of tea more.

With an effort, I heaved myself to my feet and limped in to the tiny kitchen. I popped the uneaten chips on a plate and put them in the oven to warm, clicking on the kettle as I did so.

When the tea and chips were ready, I grabbed a tray and took them into my bedroom. I put the tray on the bed, and wriggled into a plain cotton nightie. Then I got under the sheets, sitting the tray on my lap. My mind kept up a barrage of questions as I absently nibbled on my unappetising meal.

Walking all afternoon hadn't helped; hadn't shown me what to do.

I needed to do something, but what?

How?

My life of quiet study wasn't the way to resolve the feelings I still harboured for Daz. I needed to find him. I didn't know whether it was the right thing to do, but I felt the unresolved feelings for him should be faced once and for all.

How could I do that? We had long since lost contact. So what should I do?

What did people do to meet friends?

What would Daz do?

Go to the pub? Socialize? Party? Join clubs? Ride bikes?

I could no longer sit at home and feel sorry for myself, or try and think of ways to help Amy with her problems. Now I had to strike out and take on my own life in both hands and live, however hard that was going to be.

By the time I had made my decision, the rest of the chips and my cup of tea were cold. I bent over and shoved the tray onto the floor, then shimmied down into the bed. My eyes were closed and my body asleep before I had finished pulling up the blankets.

***

After three days of fretting and procrastinating, I realised I had to seek someone's help. Amy was my closest friend and yet I hesitated to call her. With no word from her since the day at the cafe, I was filled with nervous doubts. What would I say to her? Should I mention her mother? I thought it best if I waited to see what she might mention, if she ever got back in contact.

When I finally got up the courage to get in touch, she immediately agreed to meet me back at our favourite café.

We sat at our usual table, a silent barrier between us. I was not sure what to say, and Amy didn't appear to want to discuss 'that' day. The friendship had undergone a change. The letter from her Mother that I had read and the subsequent silence between us had taken its toll.

I wondered if she was still seeing the man she had met that day. I tried to remember his name. David? No! Darren? No, that wasn't it either.

I sat looking at Amy. We hadn't really struck up much of a conversation, other than to make small talk. It showed how much our friendship had changed.

I wondered if she had heard from her mother, but didn't dare broach the subject.

Amy fiddled with the sugar container on the table, and waited for me to speak. The murmur of the café's customers sounded loud in my ears. I asked if she was all right, and she merely nodded. I tentatively told her what I hoped to do.

"What?" She had lifted the cup to her lips. Now she put it down rapidly, nearly choking on her mouthful of coffee.

She grabbed a paper serviette and wiped her mouth. "My God, you want to find Daz? Come on, Clare! You've got to be joking!" She shook her head at me in disbelief.

When I asked what I should do, and if she would help, she laughed.

"Can't see you going down to the pub and drinking till you're pie-eyed! That's the only way you'll ever get Daz to even look at you - if you could find him. I wouldn't be at all surprised if he isn't married to the local sleaze, and is sufferin' with a half dozen kids by now!"

She rolled her eyes and swore.

"Mind you, your idea of finding him at the local pub probably has merit - that'd be where you'd find him. Getting pissed out of his mind, no doubt, tryin' to find a girl to lay before goin' home to the missus. Or else, tryin' to get away from his missus and kids, I reckon!!"

I felt flattened. I started to defend Daz, but when Amy looked at me with eyes full of disappointment and ridicule; I stuttered to a stop and bent my head to drink my own coffee. Any hope that Amy would help was evidently a vain hope.

"Right," I said through gritted teeth. "Thanks. Thanks for nothing!"

Now I was more determined to show her I wasn't a wimp, a nerd or a geek.

I got up and walked away. It seemed I was on my own, because the next thing I heard was her calling out.

"Hey, Damien. Come and sit down. What do you reckon? Can you see my friend, 'Studious Clare', the Uni student, going to the pub?"

Her laughter echoed in my head as I left the café. Yes – that was his name. So she was still with Damien. I wondered vaguely where he had been while we had been talking, but my anger pushed the question away.

I'd show her! If she thought I was a pushover, she could damn well think again!!

Chapter 3.

I stood in front of the mirror in the bathroom and began to apply some eye-shadow. My hand froze in position and I looked at my reflection. My stomach seemed to turn over, and small beads of perspiration glistened on my forehead. What was I doing? Who was that woman in the mirror?

I took a deep breath and blew out a stream of air, hoping my roiling stomach would settle, but I shook the doubts and negative thoughts away and continued, determinedly. If I wanted to find Daz, then this is what I had to do.

Today, as they say, was the first day of the rest of my life.

When I had finished, I walked back into my bedroom. The full-length mirror bounced another image back at me. It just wasn't me.

The dress clung to all the places that I had never worried about showing off before. The colour was a deep blue, and accented the colour of my eyes. I had twirled my long brown hair up into an untidy sort of chignon, and poked a silver stick up through it like a weaver stitching a rough seam. I glanced at my shoes and almost smiled through my nerves.

Nooooo!

Slippers were not the correct fashionable accessory for the ensemble. I opened my wardrobe and rummaged around until I found a pair of heels that I had bought for the final dance at school.

I squeezed my feet into them. Surely my feet hadn't got bigger in such a short time? I winced when I took a step - I had refused to go to the dance, so these stilettos had never been worn. I knew I would suffer until the leather had softened and moulded itself around the shape of my foot.

I took a couple more steps, testing out my balance, then lifted my chin and decided to forget the pain. I grabbed my handbag and the keys and left the flat before I could change my mind.

When I arrived at the 'Royal', the pub closest to my home, I stood outside for a while, getting up the courage to enter. The bar where the men drank was off-limits, and I was nervous about going into the 'Ladies Lounge' by myself. I'd never been inside such a place, and didn't quite know how to behave.

I gingerly went to the door and peered inside. There weren't many people inside, although I could hear the clamour of male voices from the bar along the north side of the building. I pushed the doors, and I was in - I couldn't turn around now.

I realised very quickly that I was way over-dressed for this excursion into the unknown. This wasn't a posh restaurant, and the couple of ladies sitting over by the wall, with glasses in front of them on the table, were casually dressed. I felt like a peacock in a magpie enclosure.

I sat down in the nearest chair and tried to look unconcerned, as if I was waiting for someone.

I don't think I fooled a soul. I could see the women over by the wall looking at me, then, with a raised eyebrow or two, they continued their conversation.

I was beginning to feel completely out of my depth. I knew I had to appear as if I was used to the situation, so I needed a drink in front of me, although where I could get one, I had no idea.

There was a burst of laughter from the bar, and two men came blundering into the room. They came to a stop, one bumping into the back of the other, and looked around the room in what seemed to be a bit of a haze. The women in the Ladies Lounge stopped talking and stared at them, and what had been a quiet hum of activity became a stillness, an expectant hush. The silence froze the air.

With unerring idiocy, they both looked at me. I swallowed with nervousness, imagining the gulp could be heard outside in the street. I couldn't retreat anywhere, so I just sat, looking like a dandified scarecrow.

"Hi, love," The taller of the two said, his voice slurring into his grin. "Wanna drink?"

"Are ya' by yourself?" the other man leered.

I didn't know what to do - I felt hamstrung with indecision. I looked at my hands that were clenching and unclenching on the table in front of me as if they belonged to someone else.

Before I could think of what to say, the short guy plonked down onto the seat opposite me and leaned into my space.

"Come on, love," he breathed out and the stale beery smell wafted across the table. "We only want to be friends. What's ya' fee?"

I cleared my throat, and took a breath. I had no idea what to do, but I knew I had to do something.

A feminine hand appeared on the beer-smelling man's shoulder. The tall guy giggled.

"Listen, you two no-good idiots," a woman's voice said. "Leave the lady alone - you're drunk!"

I looked up with gratitude. One of the ladies I'd noticed earlier from the table by the wall, stood behind the man seated opposite me. The taller guy still giggled like an intoxicated hyena.

"Go'orn, Dave, take your beery friend away and leave us alone." she said to the taller of the two. "We don't want your type in here." She gave them both a push as the short guy stood, knocking over the chair he had been sitting on.

"Git!" She gave the guy another shove, and he stumbled as he bumped into his mate. Both of the men whispered loudly as they left. I'm sure I heard something about 'money being offered' and 'wasn't that the idea?'

I was frowning when she turned to me.

"Hi, I'm Shirl," she smiled. "You okay?"

I let out a breath in a rush. My head was swirling and I thought I might faint.

"Thanks," I said faintly, then cleared my throat and said with more confidence. "Hi. I'm Clare."

"Well come over and join me and me friend - she's Bev."

I got up on weak and trembling legs, wishing I'd worn more sensible shoes, and followed her to the wall.

"Here," she indicated the chair, then turned to her friend. "This here's Clare," she said as she grabbed the empty glasses and asked Bev, turning and including me in the question. "What do ya want to drink?"

I had no idea what was the coolest drink in this type of situation, so I smiled and said. "Whatever! I'll have what you're having."

When she came back, three drinks were put on the table. "Hope ya' like scotch and dry," she said with a wink to her friend.

I didn't miss the wink. Were they having a go at me? Was I walking into a situation that was going to be worse than before? Did they really want to be friends, or was I just some sort of a joke, or a project to work on?

I sat down and picked up the drink.

"Thanks," I said, taking a sip. It took all my control to keep a smile on my face when I felt like grimacing. Not my idea of a pleasant drink.

Both of the women were looking at me with interest. Bev spoke.

"Nice to meet ya', Clare. Are ya' waiting for anyone?"

This was my chance.

"Yeah," I frowned. "I think I got the wrong end of the invitation, tho'. I'm sure Daz said he was coming to this spot tonight."

"Who's Daz?" Shirl asked.

"Oh. Sorry." I blinked and took another sip of the fizz in my glass. A piece of ice hit my front tooth sending a lightning spear of pain up into my skull. I put my hand to my face.

"Ow. Ice headache!" I managed to get out while thinking furiously what my next comment would be.

"Eew," Bev wrinkled her nose. "Not nice!"

I waited a moment until the pain receded.

"Daz is a friend from school - we were hoping to meet up and remember some of the good times!"

"So why the glamour togs?" Shirl asked.

I grinned.

"Might as well knock his eyes out if I can - I was always a bit of a nerd at school, while he was the 'bad boy' that was popular with the 'in crowd'."

The women laughed.

"Good for you," Bev giggled.

Shirl shook her head.

"Well, I don't think this is the pub he normally comes to - never heard of him. There's another pub down the road a bit. Maybe that was it."

"Thanks, Shirl. I'll try again later." I finished the drink and stood up.

"Before ya' go," Shirl continued. "It's your shout!"

I obviously looked a little confused because she sniffed and added." Hey, I paid for the last round - it's your turn." she glanced at Bev. "Ya' finished, or do ya' want another one?"

Bev drained the glass and nearly shattered it as it made contact with the table.

"Yep," she firmed her lips and looked at me with raised eyebrows. "One for the road, I reckon." then she smiled. "And when ya' go to meet up with ya' friend, I'd wear something a little less classy! Ya' look like a pork chop in a synagogue! Too high class for this scene! - you'll frighten 'im off."

I pulled out a two dollar note and gently placed it in front of Shirl.

"Look, I'm going to try the other hotel," I said. "Here, hope this is enough!" and with that I turned and walked out of the Ladies Lounge with as much dignity as my four- inch heels and the dizziness from the unaccustomed scotch and dry and the remains of the headache, would allow me. What Shirl and Bev thought of me was none of my concern, but at least I'd got some information now to help in my next foray into the pub scene.

***

It took me a week to get up the courage to try again. I'd gone to the local second-hand clothing store and found a few inexpensive clothes that I thought might be better suited to the pub crowd. I had them laid out on my bed trying to decide what to wear this time.

In the end, I picked out a short black mini skirt and a sparkly top in a bright pink. I popped some dangly ear-rings in my newly pierced ears and some platform shoes on my feet. I was still unsure if they were going to be easier to walk on, but concluded that they were much more stable than the stiletto heels I had worn before.

The hotel on the main road was a lot less daunting than the first. I now knew to go to the lounge area, and walk in with confidence. I saw the counter where I could order a drink and made my way straight to it.

"Can I have a shandy?" I asked the waiter.

"That'll be 50 cents," he said, looking me up and down with a slight hint of disapproval as he passed the chilled glass of beer and lemonade towards me.

I took the glass, left the money and turned to search for a vacant table. The only place I could see to sit was a spare chair at a table with a couple who appeared to be husband and wife.

I sauntered over.

"Do you mind if I sit here?" I asked.

The couple stopped and looked at me.

"Um," the man hesitated. "We're expecting a friend. Sorry."

"Oh!" I smiled, still glancing around to see if I could find a seat. "Okay. No problem." I had no idea where I could have the drink, as well as find out if this might be where Daz came in his spare time. How was I going to find out?

Suddenly a group of laughing girls got up and left the room in a burst of energy. I made my way to the table and sat down. One of the girls turned and ran back in and I saw that a cardigan was still on the back of one of the chairs. I reached over and took it off, handing it to the girl as she arrived at the table.

"Yours?" I asked.

"Yeah, nearly forgot it." she said with a smile as she took it from my hand. "Thanks." She stood and looked at me.

"Aren't you Amy's friend?"

"Um... yes."

I suddenly realized I hadn't spoken to Amy since the incident in the café, when I had asked for her help. This time I had to admit that I had not thought of her – the friendship had finished, but I discovered I was still concerned. Had something happened to her? Was she okay? Had her Mum come back? Oh my goodness, had Amy done something silly?

"She alright?" I asked, feeling a little silly that I even had to ask.

"Yeah," the girl answered. "She's going out with a new bloke, so none of us get a look-in at the moment." she dismissed the thought and pulled out the closest chair and perched on the edge. "Thought you went to Uni?"

"Yeah," I nodded. "I'm here looking for an old friend from school."

"Who?"

"Do you know Daz? I asked."

One of the girls that had been at the table poked her head around the exit door.

"You coming, Brenda? We're all waiting."

Brenda turned from me and yelled.

"Coming!"

She stood up, shrugged the cardigan over her shoulders then turned to me.

"Daz frequents the White Horse pub in the next suburb. If you're going to walk home, be careful - the clothes you're wearing might give the local bikey gangs the wrong idea."

She left before I could answer. I looked down at the expanse of white thigh that the mini skirt revealed, and thought she might have been right. I'd have to find some more respectable clothes next time. Seems I was too posh at the first pub, and now too casual at this hotel. Somewhere in between was obviously the look I should aim for.

Chapter 4.

I didn't stay much longer after that. My thoughts centred on only two things. Firstly I had to find the White Horse hotel, and secondly what had Brenda really meant when she had said my clothes gave the wrong idea?

The walk home wasn't far, but it took me past several semi-detached housing commission homes. I could hear couples bickering, children screaming and the occasional television blaring. The street pavement was uneven, and weeds often crept through the fences of neglected gardens and made the path an obstacle course. The number of street lights that had been broken out-numbered the ones that worked, so the street was dim.

I really didn't notice. I walked along in a dream, thinking about the real possibility that I would soon see Daz again. As the moments passed, the wind began to gust, and the temperature dropped. I began to hurry as I had not brought a jacket with me and I was getting cold. Another fifteen minutes and I would be in the cosiness of my own flat.

As I began to move faster, I became aware of footsteps behind me, and the raucous and taunting sound of several male voices. It sent a warning tingle down my back, but I didn't turn around and look. This seemed to be happening to me too often, and I had to stop reacting to sounds that were part of a normal neighbourhood.

The platform shoes caught on a crack in the pavement, causing my right foot to twist, and I fell onto the path. I didn't need the delay. I tried desperately to convince myself that my fear was silly and that I was being overly cautious. I had felt the same fear before and it had only been a boy hurrying home. My mind relaxed a little. I rubbed my foot and tried to stand.

Suddenly I was surrounded.

"Damn! This must be a new kid on the block," a long lanky guy with a greasy hairdo said to the others.

"Well, Billy, you don't intend to pay for the use, do ya'?" asked another. The gang roared with laughter, and one skinny boy came forward, to stand over me with his hands on his hips.

"Don't look as if she's going anywhere in a hurry, but it'll be much more fun if we hold her down for ya' before we have our turn."

Billy grinned. "Yeah, always liked an audience. It's going to be extra enjoyable with this one. She was always a stuck-up bitch."

The skinny one bent down and grabbed my arm, yanking me towards the hedge of a nearby ramshackle house with an equally neglected garden. The fear over-rode my thoughts but I vaguely connected the name of the man standing over me, leering, with the boy from my year in school. Surely it wasn't the same Billy that Amy had drooled over? I didn't have the chance to follow that thought as the guy holding my arm kicked me casually in the stomach. Pain obliterated any reason and I screamed. A hand came down hard across my face and strangled the sound as it pressed my head to the ground, covering my mouth and nearly pushing my teeth down my throat.

"Do ya' want her kickin' and screamin' or beaten and quiet?" he asked as the rest of the males surged forward.

"I don't want her making a noise, but a bit of fight always gets me going," Billy said, and the rest of them agreed. The skinny one hit me across the face again, and I felt blood trickle down my chin.

"If ya' know what's good for yer, yer'll keep quiet, and let us sample ya' goods before Billy hits ya' till ya' can't speak!" He thrust me back down on the ground as I tried to struggle to my feet and I felt gravel tear at my limbs. My arms were held in check by a guy on each side, while another grabbed my legs and pulled them apart.

"Hey, Billy - look at this?" He said. "She's got red knickers on."

"Tear 'em off - I'm ready and as hard as a stick - let me at her."

I tried to fight, to kick and scream, but nothing happened. My mouth was swollen and my limbs were held in a steel grip. The sound of my knickers tearing made me want to scream but the hand across my mouth had partially covered my nose and I was struggling to breathe.

I caught a glimpse of my red pants being hoisted into the air and waved about as the boys on each leg pulled them harder apart. I felt as if I would tear in half. The pain blurred my eyes with tears and the sound of their maniacal laughter dimmed until my whole world became pain and embarrassment.

I could feel tears of fear and rage slipping across my cheeks as I lay visible to the world and bleeding from the scratches and the punches that kept raining upon me every time I struggled.

My knickers disappeared from view as my short skirt was lifted around my waist. Someone had torn my top to expose my breasts, and a hot, slobbery mouth was half biting at them.

Just as I expected the worse, everything went into slow motion, and I was released. I heard the men scramble to their feet and Billy told them to run.

I didn't move.

I couldn't.

The pain was intense. I hurt from my toes to my forehead. My face felt twice its size. I managed to close my legs, and wrap my arms across my bare chest, and then I don't remember any more.

***

When I awoke, the glare of lights nearly blinded me. I really didn't want to open my eyes. Every bone and muscle in my body felt as if it had been stretched and broken. I could hear movement around me, and I felt a warm hand clutch mine.

"I'm here," a male voice whispered near my ear.

I shuddered. Had the gang still got me? Where was I? Who was holding my hand?

I tried to snatch it away, but my body wouldn't obey my thoughts.

"Shh - It's OK!" The voice continued.

I forced my eyes to open, and saw the white of the ceiling. Tears were slipping down the side of my face, and there was something warm tucked around me. It wasn't until I saw a woman smile at me from above that I finally understood that I was in hospital.

I relaxed for a brief instant, until my brain screamed at me - who was the man with me?

I cautiously turned my head. A stranger was beside my bed, and he was smiling through concerned eyes.

I frowned in puzzlement.

"Who....? How....?"

"Shh, shh," he said. "You're safe now. I found you before they could hurt you anymore."

"But..."

"No, don't talk - you need your strength to get over the beating you got. I'll explain later. Close your eyes and rest."

Again, I succumbed to the painful weariness and slept.

***

When I awoke next, I kept my eyes closed and listened. I couldn't hear anything except the normal noises of the hospital. I was frightened to move, in case I hurt, so I didn't. With as much control as I could muster, I slowly turned my head towards the right, opening my eyes fractionally to see if I was alone. The corridor was brilliantly lit, and the dazzle made my eyes sting. I closed them again quickly.

I had not seen anyone in that brief second of sight, so I began to relax my tense muscles.

"Ah! You're awake."

I must have physically jumped, because a hand settled on my left arm and rubbed gently, as if to soothe me.

"Don't worry, I'm still here," the man's voice murmured.

This time I turned and stared at the person sitting on my left.

"Who are you?" My voice sounded gravelly in my ears.

The man smiled. It crinkled up his hazel eyes and lifted his stubbly cheeks. I vaguely wondered if he was going for a new fashionable look, or if he had been next to me so long that he had not been able to shave.

"I'm Steve, and I helped you the other night."

"Oh!" I felt my cheeks burn as I remembered how I must have looked when he had found me.

"I'm so pleased I had decided to go for a walk," he continued. "I was able to shout 'Cops' and frighten away those bast..." He caught the word in his throat and I could hear the emotion as it rose up to choke him. "Thankfully they didn't realize I was bluffing. Fortunately I was just in time, before they could do anything more to you. I'm sorry I couldn't stop the punches they landed on you before I got there."

I nodded.

"Thank you, Steve." I murmured, already feeling weary again. "How long have you been here?"

Steve shook his head. I could see the tiredness in his face as he patted my arm reassuringly.

"Don't worry about me," he said. "You just rest and relax. Concentrate on getting better."

A nurse came bustling in pushing a trolley.

"Hello, Steve," she said. "Now that she's awake, give us a few moments, please, while I do the check."

Steve stood. He looked at me. "I'll come back shortly," he said "and we can talk. I'll go and have a coffee." He gave another squeeze of my hand and walked out of the ward.

After the nurse had taken my temperature, checked my blood pressure and changed and removed some of the dressings on the gravel rash, she left the room. I was frustrated. Why wouldn't they tell me what was happening?

A moment later the head nurse walked in.

"Hi, Clare."

How had they learnt my name?

When she saw me frown, she smiled.

"You are going to have to thank Steve. He collected the contents of your handbag that those louts had scattered all over the place."

She continued as I tried a weak smile. Did everyone know about my humiliation? How could they be so kind to me – they must think I am terrible to allow the outrage that happened. The nurse kept smiling as she unclipped the board at the end of the bed and glanced down at the report there.

"Ah good," she commented. "Everything appears normal. The police will be here to interview you. You'll be able to go home after that."

She must have seen the look of sheer panic in my eyes, because she continued, "Don't worry. The police want you to remember as much as you can. This is the third rape case in the area this month. Lucky for you Steve came by when he did - he saved you from more injury and stopped the intended rape before it happened. The other two girls weren't so lucky. So, the police are anxious to get as much information as they possibly can get to try and stop this particular gang."

I swallowed nervously. I didn't want to re-live the experience, but knew the gang had to be stopped.

"Do you want me to sit in with you?" the nurse asked. "Or would you prefer Steve to be here?"

"Could you be here?" I asked shyly. "I've only just met Steve, and I would be too embarrassed to talk in front of him."

"Okay, no problem. The police will want to talk to him anyway, so when they arrive, I'll be here."

"Thank you."

"As soon as the interview is over, we'll organize your discharge. Steve has already offered to take you home. Is that all right?"

I nodded. "I'll speak to him about that when he comes back," I promised.

As if he had heard my last remark, Steve came in to the room as the nurse left.

"Everything OK?" he said.

"Mmm." I wasn't sure what to say next.

He seemed to know what I was thinking.

"The police will be kind, you know. This wasn't your fault. I'll tell them what I saw, too."

Tears threatened again, and I blinked them away. Before I could say anything, he sat down, held my hand and sighed.

"I'm so pleased I found you," he said once more. "When they let you out of here, I'll be honoured to take you to your home, if you'll let me."

How could I refuse? He had been nothing but a friend to me during this ordeal. Although he was still a new acquaintance I knew he would be offended if I said no.

"I ..."

He interrupted. "If you'd rather someone else, I won't be offended," he offered, as if he'd heard me.

"No," I smiled, even though it hurt my face and reminded me that the bruises were still fresh. "That's ok. That would be lovely."

"What about your family?" he asked.

"No ... don't tell them. I don't want them to know. I'll be all right." I turned my face away. I was already aware how I must look - with swollen eyes, bruised cheeks and a split lip. The gravel wounds on my back and the bruises on my body were sore. I had no idea why Steve had stayed around for so long. I must have looked terrible.

Once again we were interrupted, as the head nurse and two police officers entered the room.

"Please leave us, sir," one of the police directed their attention to Steve. "We'll speak with you shortly. If you wouldn't mind waiting in the room down the corridor on the left, we will see you shortly."

Steve gave me an apologetic type of smile and left.

The nurse sat next to me while the two police officers stood at the end of the bed.

"Ok," The older of the two spoke first. "You're name is Clare Simpson. Is that correct?"

I nodded. I wasn't looking forward to the next few minutes. So many people considered that attempted rape was always the woman's fault, and I didn't know whether this would be how the police thought as well.

The interview was as I expected. I was worn out at the end, with doubts as to my innocence, and emotional at the recalling of the incident. The police were impersonal and businesslike. I was so glad the head nurse had been at my side throughout the questioning. She had been a tower of strength and interrupted them a couple of times with a righteous type of disapproval, as if she was my mother. When the police finally finished, I wanted to get out of the hospital and get home as soon as I could. As the police walked away I heard one of them say - 'Must have been asking for it, if you ask me.' The answer was lost as they turned a bend in the corridor.

I was so embarrassed. I hadn't done anything, as far as I knew, that would have encouraged the attack. I didn't know whether to be angry or not. Had I sent the wrong signals? Was I asking to be mauled and denigrated, humiliated and assaulted? I was confused, still sore and, no doubt, still in shock. If only I was at home. To relax in my own surroundings, with a cup of tea and a comfortable and quiet bed sounded like heaven.

It was another hour and a half before the discharge papers were ready and I had gingerly got out of bed and dressed to go home. Finally, Steve arrived and escorted me downstairs to check out and helped me into his car, and I was on my way home.

As Steve concentrated on the driving, I tried to erase the pictures in my head of the events leading to this point. I'd told the police that the only name I remembered was Billy, and that he seemed to be the boss. But the violation I felt having my body opened up to the eyes of strangers, including Steve beside me, was impossible to forget. Every time I closed my eyes, I saw the youths that held me down, and I still felt the slobber of the mouth that had been on my breast.

I worried that the images would never go away. I worried how I was going to react when Steve came into my home and we were alone. I worried about when Steve left and I was on my own with those pictures. I worried about telling my parents what had happened. I worried about not telling my parents. I worried about Amy and our friendship, but I didn't want her to know either. Yet I felt that I needed someone to help me over the trauma. Was there anyone I would trust to tell? Was there anyone who could help?

When Steve parked the car, I couldn't move. I was still, in my mind, lying on the ground trying to pretend the assault wasn't occurring.

"Clare?"

I shook away the horror and looked at Steve. He was holding out his hand and waiting for me to take it. I did so and got out of the car and let him lead me inside my flat. I seemed to be on autopilot, and felt strangely robot like.

Inside, I sat down and looked around me. Why wasn't everything different? My world had been shattered, my innocence broken and my confidence wrecked. The room, though, looked the same.

"Clare? Where do you keep your tea and sugar?" Steve's voice drifted toward me from the kitchen. "Oh! Never mind, I've found it."

It seemed like he immediately placed a hot cup of tea beside me.

"Thanks," I said. "Did you sugar it?"

"Yep," he grinned. "Milk and one sugar - just how you like it."

I glanced up at him.

"How...?"

"You told me in the hospital before we left! You told me all you wanted was a nice cup of tea and a comfortable bed!"

I vaguely remembered the conversation now that he mentioned it, and told him so.

While he made sure that I drank, he made some toast and jam and sat down next to me.

"Now, are you well enough to talk?"

I felt so weary that I was almost in tears, but I heard myself tell him I was OK.

"I don't think so," he smiled reassuringly. "It will help to talk it out. I won't mind. I'm a good listener."

It was all I needed. We sat for what seemed hours and I spewed out all my troubles. Steve sat quietly, and I kept talking, letting out the grief and fear that I suffered. He held me when I cried; he wiped my tears, and held my hand. I found that I could tell him things about myself that I had never even admitted to myself, let alone a stranger. I told him about Daz. I told him that I loved my school-time sweetheart, and that I wanted to find him.

Steve listened, Steve comforted and Steve offered to help.

Then he suggested that, as a friend, he would stay the night on the couch while I got some sleep. That he would be there if the night brought nightmares with it. He smiled as he settled onto the lounge, and sent me off to bed telling me not to worry.

If only it was that easy.

***

It took several days before I could close my eyes in some semblance of peace. Steve visited every day and listened to me say the same things over and over again without once losing patience with me. Without him as a friend, I don't know if I would have coped.

I gave my lectures up for the week - there was no point turning up when I would have never been able to focus. I knew that tears were still just below the surface, and I would have been horrified if I had lost control at University. Having decided previously to find Daz before I worried about finishing the course, it didn't really matter, anyway.

By the following week, I felt brave enough to escape my self-imposed imprisonment, and I walked to the local shop for some fresh food.

I still felt vulnerable.

I jumped at shadows.

Every male who walked towards me made my heart race with anxiety, but I kept walking. I faced my fears and nothing happened. The local fruit and vegetable store was crowded, but I bought some apples, and smiled at the man behind the counter.

"That'll be 50c," he said, waiting for me to pay. He didn't even look at me with curiosity. I gave him the coins and he thanked me.

"Have a nice day," he murmured as he turned to look at the next customer.

I got home and sat down on the sofa, exhausted from my excursion. I felt as if I had run a marathon, but I was happy. I had taken my first step to getting back to a normal life.

When Steve came by that evening, I told him of my success. He was really pleased. I didn't mention that I still felt the horror of the experience whenever I was alone. How I fought the fear inside; the trembling, the images and the embarrassment that would wash over me at unusual moments and that still sometimes became too much to bear.

"The next thing we should do is go out and celebrate." he suggested

I wasn't so sure. I didn't think I was ready for that. It felt like a huge step. Going out at night was the last thing I wanted to do.

Steve must have seen the panic flare in my eyes.

"I will be with you," he added. "We'll go out to a nice restaurant where there are no crowds."

I nodded, but my stomach had turned over and I felt sick.

***

Steve was patient. He waited until I felt that I could fight the demons of darkness outside the safety of my flat.

A month passed.

I dressed in a conservative skirt and twinset, brushed my hair until it shone and hesitantly put a pair of tiny earrings in my ears. When Steve knocked on the door and I opened it he smiled.

"You look lovely," he remarked, holding out his hand to escort me to the car.

I hesitated. Steve waited. I took a deep breath and stepped out of my self-imposed sanctuary.

To get to the restaurant, Steve drove. The night was exceptionally dark and the traffic heavy. It took us thirty minutes to arrive and I sat in silence. Steve didn't appear to notice as he concentrated on the road.

The restaurant was on the outskirts of town, and had a small car park. The parking area was surrounded by trees, and the owners of 'The Gourmet Duck Inn' had created beautiful gardens edging the bays. When we parked the car, Steve held my hand and led me into a calm, dimly lit room that oozed luxury. I stood transfixed as Steve organized our table seating. The walls were a muted shade of peach, and artwork was judiciously placed around the area so as not to overpower the ambience of the large space. Several tables ran along the edge of the room, each by a window, with movable curtains around them to secure some privacy.

This was not some cheap and nasty diner, or greasy pub cafeteria. This spoke money, and I was overawed.

It made me realize that I had no idea what Steve did for a living when he was away from me. I had been so selfish, using his friendly shoulders and infinite wisdom to unburden myself and try to heal. Not once had I enquired about his family, his feelings and his thoughts. I knew virtually nothing beyond the open friendship he had offered.

When we sat, I didn't know what to say. What if he was married? The thought hadn't occurred to me before. What if he was some sort of female predator? I shook my head inwardly. That was ridiculous. He had been polite and charming right from the start. He had never made me feel uncomfortable. Even so, my confidence and my self-esteem were low, and I didn't know if I could trust myself, let alone him however nice he had been.

Steve handed me the menu, and I used it to cover my confusion. We ordered. The meal consisted of an entree of oysters, then steak and salad – finishing with a dessert of pavlova and ice-cream. It was delicious. Steve continued to keep up the conversation and I never got around to asking him for the information.

The night was pleasant, but tiring, so when we arrived back at my flat, I begged Steve to leave me so I could collapse into bed.

The celebratory meal helped me move on and in the next few weeks I ventured outside a little more each day. Steve was still there, but his visits were becoming less frequent.

I began to think once more about my mission to find Daz.

Several weeks after the gang's attack, I broached the subject again with Steve. I hadn't heard from Amy, and I certainly hadn't told my parents about the trouble I had had. I'd been back at University for a while, and we were due to have a break before the next semester. It seemed the perfect time to put my fears away and continue my search.

"Are you sure?" Steve asked.

"Yes." I had already told Steve about Daz and the schoolgirl crush that I had experienced and the relationship that had ensued. I was determined to follow through and see if Daz could still make my heart flutter and my knees go weak!

"Ok! Then I will help. Where shall we start?"

We started at the last hotel that I had been to before the attack. I couldn't remember the name of the hotel that the girl who had rescued her cardigan had mentioned.

We entered the ladies lounge. I couldn't see anyone I knew, and this time there were plenty of seats. I sat down, smoothing my skirt down as I turned to Steve.

"I wonder whether I could have a lemon squash?" I asked. My stomach was clenched unexpectedly with nerves rather from the excitement I wished I felt.

Steve went to get us something to drink. In the relative quiet of the early afternoon, before the rush of the workers arriving at the bar, I heard Steve speak.

"Just wondering," he commented to another guy who was lounging on the bar. "Is there another pub around here that has a name of an animal? Horse, I think?"

The man stubbed out a cigarette and grabbed his schooner of beer.

"Not as good as this pub," he drawled. "'The White Horse' over in the next suburb gets a lot of riff-raff. Don't bother goin' there - they're a bad lot!"

"Thanks, mate." Steve said as he picked up the lemon squash for me and his beer, nodding to the bartender at the same time.

"No worries," the smoker replied, already lighting another cigarette.

By the time he came back to the table I was beginning to get anxious.

"The name is 'The White Horse'," he said once he'd sat down and taken a sip of his beer.

"Of course," I smiled at him. "I remember, now." I pushed my drink away and went to stand up. "Let's go."

Steve put his hand on my arm and restrained me.

"Hang on. Let's talk about this. Don't be so impatient."

"I can't help it," I sat down again, reluctantly. "I want to see Daz as quickly as I can."

Steve shook his head. "It's not as simple as that."

"Why?" I interjected.

"The guy I spoke to at the bar told me it wasn't a very reputable pub."

"So?" I didn't understand the problem.

"Tut, tut!" Steve smiled to take the sting out of his words. "You are too innocent! You don't want to walk in to the same thing that happened to you before!"

I cringed. Definitely not, but I hadn't thought about it. I just wanted to see Daz again.

"Now," Steve continued when he saw I had settled down a little. "We've got to plan this time." He paused. "Finish your drink. Enjoy the evening, then I'll take you home and we can discuss what we need to do."

I gulped down the rest of my drink. I was too tense with excitement now to stay.

"OK. Done. Let's go."

Steve leant back on his chair.

"I'm not rushing - I want to enjoy my time out with you, and actually taste my drink!"

I glowered at him, and sat down, tension oozing from every pore. Too stressed to sit still, but forced to wait.

***

We went to the 'The White Horse' some two days later. I very nearly went by myself as soon as Steve had taken me home, discussed a plan then had left - telling me to rest.

The only reason I didn't take matters into my own hands was the dread of the unknown and the images that kept flashing in my mind from the attack. I needed Steve there as my back-up.

When we walked into 'The White Horse' lounge, it was immediately obvious that this was a more raucous crowd. The noise levels, even in the ladies lounge, didn't cover the swearing, catcalls and fighting words that streamed out of the bar.

Steve offered to go in and get the drinks.

"You stay here," he said. "Don't stare at anyone or smile. Keep cool and try and be patient. I won't be long."

As he walked away, I felt vulnerable and a little scared. Two girls at the next table were having what appeared to be an argument. On the other side, a group of women was having a loud party. I sat quietly, feeling completely out of my depth. Nobody took any notice of me. A couple of girls got up and disappeared into the 'ladies', and a handful of men came out of the bar area with handfuls of brimming glasses. They put them down at what I presumed was their girlfriend's tables and promptly returned to the bar.

I kept watching the door to the bar for Steve. Every time the door opened and the noise percolated into the lounge I tensed a bit more.

I sighed with relief when Steve finally returned, clutching our drinks.

He sat down.

"Here."

He pushed the orange juice towards me.

"I got you this instead of lemon squash," he grinned. "It looks like a vodka and orange!"

I tried to smile through the stress. It probably looked more like a grimace.

"A lemon squash could have been a gin and lemon," I said.

"True," Steve chuckled. "Relax, girl! I think I'll get you a straight scotch next time! That will make your toes curl and take the frightened rabbit look off your face!"

I gave him a 'sorry-I'm-so-tense' type grin and lowered my head. I needed to get rid of the butterflies in my stomach and calm myself.

"Do you want to know what I found out?"

My head came back up so quickly I nearly snapped my teeth together. I stared at Steve with anticipation. He laughed.

"Oh dear," he shook his head. "You're tighter than a fat lady's belt!"

He drank his beer.

"Well?"

If I could have got up and gone around the table and shaken him without getting arrested, I would have.

He took another mouthful of beer.

"Daz comes here every Wednesday night after work. Apparently he's not well liked in this pub, but he comes in with a load of workmates, so they put up with him."

I frowned.

"I wonder why? He used to be the most popular boy in school!"

"Are you sure that was not just your take on it?" Steve asked. "You did tell me you thought the sun shone out of him!"

I grinned.

"Yeah - well I suppose I could be a bit biased!"

"OK. Now we have to make a plan for next Wednesday evening!" Steve proceeded to drink the dregs of his beer. "Do you want another drink?" he asked. "I'm going to get myself another one and I might be able to get a bit more information."

I looked at my half-finished orange juice.

"No thanks, I'm fine."

Steve came back in a short while with another beer.

"Another little snippet of info." He said. I leaned forward in anticipation.

"Yes?"

"He seems to be a bit of a flirt with the ladies, and has often disappeared for the night with one of them. The guy who told me said it was his girlfriend last time. He'll 'steal' any girl from even his friends, so that's why he is not liked very much."

"Oh! Is that all. Must mean he's still single then."

Steve shrugged.

"Not necessarily!"

That wasn't what I wanted to hear. I glared at Steve with as much disapproval as I could put into the look.

Chapter 5.

Although Steve said he would come with me on the following Wednesday night, he promised to stay in the background, only making his presence felt if he thought I was in trouble.

When Wednesday arrived I was so excited that I hadn't been able to sit still all day. By evening, I was in a dilemma. I had three different outfits laid out on my bed. I didn't know what to wear that would be 'just right'. I wanted to knock Daz's eyes out, but I didn't want to appear easy, like the outfit that I had worn that had seemed to cause the attack previously.

I finally chose a sedate, but figure-hugging green shift that I could dress up with some of my costume jewellery.

I spent at least two hours getting ready, putting make-up on and doing my hair.

When Steve arrived and I opened the door, he let out a low whistle.

"Weeee...ll. Clare, you look lovely."

I closed my eyes and smiled. I must have got it right this time.

"Thanks," I sighed.

"No worries," Steve said. I really didn't understand the look on his face, and the tenseness in his attitude. I was too caught up with the exhilaration of finally hoping tonight was the night my life would take on a new direction.

"Let's go, then."

I almost pushed him out of the way as I ran past him to get into his car. It never occurred to me that Steve was finding my obsession with Daz something of a difficulty. I never heard the sigh as he turned and followed me to his car.

We arrived at the hotel early, before the influx of the working men. I sat and fidgeted in the Ladies Lounge, drinking quickly and nervously. Steve kept telling me to settle down. He had talked to me about him going into the bar to find Daz, and bringing him out to me, but I was now so tied up in knots, that I worried that we had got it all wrong, and that Daz would not be at the bar at all.

When the noise level in the bar increased, we knew the men had arrived.

Steve got up.

"Now," he hesitated, and held my hand briefly, looking into my eyes with concern. "I'll go and find this Daz of yours. Please try and calm down, and don't look quite so eager to meet him."

I nodded, giving him a quick jittery smile. He patted me on the shoulder as he left.

I sat, staring at the door to the bar. In the last few months, some women had started to join the men in the bar area. They were termed 'loose' women by a lot of respectable members of society so I hesitated and wondered if I would dare to go in. I couldn't get up the courage. The rules of society kept me sitting in the lounge.

I remained stuck. I was so anxious to see Daz, but I was too scared to appear too forward with my behaviour. I spent the time thinking I had probably made a mistake coming.

What should I say if Daz came out? What if he didn't come out? What if he didn't want to see me? What if he didn't want to talk to me? What if he hated me? What if Steve didn't find him? What if he did? The thoughts running around and around in my mind were making me feel nauseous.

Then Daz walked into the room.

He looked around and saw me and smiled. I was so excited I froze! I'm sure I sat there with my mouth opening and closing like a guppy fish. No sound came out, and I don't think I even smiled back at him.

Before I could do anything, he had loped over to the table, plonked a glass of beer on the table and sat down.

"Well, hello, Clare!"

I still stared at him with complete surprise.

"You're the last person I expected to see, but I'm so pleased. I've often wondered if we'd ever see one another again."

I swallowed. He was still smiling. I didn't want to appear like an idiot, so I cleared my throat and put out my hand.

He grasped it and squeezed.

"Oh my God, Clare. You look so great. How are you?"

It took me what seemed forever to croak out a response.

"I'm fine. You?" the words sounded strained and senseless to my ears. I took a large mouthful of my drink, and it somehow got lodged in my throat. I started to cough. Daz dashed around and began to pat me on the back.

"Careful," he said as he pulled me up from the chair, pounded me harder on my back and wrapped his arms around me.

Tears streamed down my face. I kept thinking that I hadn't meant to look like such a dork, that my mascara must be running down my face, that I had no chance of ever seeing Daz again after my bad impression tonight. When the coughing eased and I gulped some air, I was able to see Steve over Daz's shoulder. He was hovering in the doorway by the bar.

I realized I was being hugged closely by Daz, and I melted into his body as if I was made to be there. I couldn't quite believe I was in his arms. I shut my eyes and savoured the feeling. When I opened them again Steve had disappeared.

After that, the tension in the air quickly dissipated and before another awkward episode could mar the evening Daz sat me down and ordered more drinks. Slowly the conversation began to flow and we laughed and reminisced about our school days as if they had occurred decades ago. The time passed quickly and we continued to drink. I was feeling dizzy with joy and just a little drunk, and then my evening became even better. Daz asked me out for dinner the following Saturday.

I heard myself agree, but my brain had become mush! I was so excited, I think I babbled incoherently.

Chapter 6.

From the moment I opened my eyes on Saturday morning, my stomach began to fill with a horde of butterflies. I wasn't sure whether it was from excitement, doubt or fear. The muscles were clenched so tight that I had no appetite for breakfast, no enjoyment in reading a relaxing book and no idea how I was going to sit still and wait for the evening.

I began going through my wardrobe. This was worse than deciding what to wear in case I met Daz - now I was actually going on a date with him - to dinner, no less!

My brain whirled. Where did he say we were going? I raced to the telephone directory and looked up 'Restaurants' and 'Cafés'. Maybe that would jog my memory. Was it a high class place, or a casual eatery?

Ah! Found it!

'The Little Morsel' restaurant on High Street.

Mmm? I thought I remembered it. Somewhere between an upper-class place and a greasy spoon type place.

Good! I could wear something casual yet a little classy. I grimaced with frustration when I opened my wardrobe. It held a measly collection of 'going-out' dresses. Several of my outfits were laid out on the bed, and I stood back and looked at them with critical eyes. It was hopeless. I had nothing to wear!

In the end I decided to pick the turquoise skirt, with a little beaded black top. It was a little sparkly, but I could tone it down with my pair of black flat shoes. Now all that was needed was a little clutch purse. I rummaged around in the bottom of the wardrobe amongst the shoes, bags and clutter. At last I came up for air, victorious, with a little black silk purse with a gold chain handle. It was perfect.

Would I wear my hoop earrings? I shook my head. Not classy enough.

What about my necklace with the baubles I bought at the op-shop? No – too trashy. If I'd had any pearls, that would have been too snobby. There was only one answer. No jewellery.

There.

Organized.

I looked at the clock. It was only ten o'clock in the morning. What was I going to do for the rest of the day?

I decided to call Amy. I hadn't seen her for ages, and I needed to let my girlfriend know what had been happening to me and why we hadn't spoken for ages. It would be nice to have a face to face chat and a coffee at our favourite café to take my mind off the long hours between now and this evening with Daz.

She answered on the first ring.

"Hi, Amy here."

"Hi, Amy. Clare here." and before she could speak I continued. "Sorry I haven't seen you for weeks - things have been a bit chaotic - do you want to meet up for coffee?"

There was silence for a few anxious moments. Since our last meeting the friendship had foundered and would never be the same – I was already feeling uncomfortable and I could hear Amy also felt the same.

"Um. Well, I was going to go shopping, but I can meet you for a short while. Normal spot?"

Was there a sign of disapproval in her tone? She had been my best friend for so long that it was difficult to believe the ties had been loosened. I hadn't heard from her for a long time. Was our friendship at an end? I didn't know. I couldn't tell.

With all that had happened I was fighting my own demons and fears. Perhaps I only imagined the ice in her voice?

"Yep!" I chirruped, hearing the false cheerfulness in my own voice, but not able to do anything about it. "See you in about half an hour?"

"OK," she answered. I definitely felt a slight censure and a coolness in her attitude, but dismissed it as my problem, not hers.

I threw on some slacks and a sweater and dashed out the door, arriving at the café about ten minutes early. I picked a seat by the window and waited nervously.

When Amy walked in, I knew straight away that she wasn't happy. She sat down with an audible puff of air.

"Yes - what did you want?"

I grimaced.

"Sorry, Amy. I really haven't been up to seeing people lately."

"Mmm," her lips compressed with disbelief. "That's not what I heard. I believe you've been swanning around all the local pubs with some bloke."

"You're right," I agreed. She looked at me and raised her eyebrows.

"I'll explain," I promised, and I did.

She sat quietly sipping her coffee and listened. I explained the attack, the rescue by Steve, the need to hide and then the decision to find Daz and how I'd achieved it. Finally I told her about my date tonight.

"Ok," she said at the end as I coasted to a stuttering halt. "I know that's a lot, but why didn't you let me know. I don't understand. I thought we used to be best friends."

I took a deep breath and shook my head. "I guess I was worried you wouldn't understand, and I knew you were worried about your Mum."

I wished I hadn't mentioned that, as her eyes became cold and distant. I continued with a rush, trying to cover up the gaff.

"Um - I met someone in town that said you were off doing your thing with a new boyfriend and not on our normal social scene. I didn't want to bother you."

Amy picked up her handbag.

"Look, I've got to go - the boyfriend thing has gone now anyway, I've got other fish to fry! If you want me, I'll see if I'm free. See you 'round."

She left.

I'd definitely offended her. I sat there for some time trying to come to terms with the chilly response, and wondered if we'd ever be friends again like we used to be. I had touched a raw nerve when I'd spoken about her mother, and whether she had found her. I should have realised when she completely shut the subject down, and I hadn't found out if there had been a resolution to the separation. No wonder she was angry with me. Her world had tipped upside down, too. From now on, I needed to be more supportive of others and not be so caught up with my own problems. I was getting way too selfish.

After I finished my coffee and left the café, I went straight to a florist and sent Amy some flowers with my love. It wouldn't hurt to be the first to put my hand out in friendship. I was partly at fault after all was said and done. My actions had been selfish and self-centred. I would continue to try to heal the breech that the attack had opened and keep Amy as my friend, whatever happened.

By the time I got home, it was past lunch, and as soon as I closed the door to the outside, my butterflies returned. They felt like rather large moths now. I wandered around my flat the rest of the afternoon, and when it was time to get ready for my date, it was almost a relief.

At seven o'clock sharp there was a knock at the door, and I was as nervous as a kitten. I opened the door and Daz and I just stood and looked at one another. He looked gorgeous, in a pair of tan trousers and a cream shirt, with his hair immaculately done and a look in his eyes that told me he liked what he saw, too.

"Hi," I squeaked.

"Hi," he answered, offering his arm to escort me to the car. He was charming, and I was charmed.

***

Daz courted me with an old-fashioned gallantry. We went to restaurants, to movies and to picnics in the park. He escorted me to parties, to gallery exhibitions and to musical concerts. He never put a foot wrong, and never pushed me with too much intimacy. Every time he tried to kiss me, he felt me stiffen with nerves.

"It's OK, Clare," he said, smiling at me and patting my hand. "I know you were badly shaken up by what happened, and I know it will take time for you to learn to relax with me."

I nodded. "Sorry. I so want to be loved by you. Just give me time."

"Of course," he said.

I was smitten.

Even so, I continued to meet Amy and I let her know what was happening. She didn't seem very pleased with my renewed acquaintance with Daz. During our conversations I had eventually discovered that her mother still had not contacted her, and that she didn't want to talk about it. It was a forbidden subject.

She seemed to have become even more determined to live her life on the edge. She had been going out with a guy called Graham, and then it was Don. Now it was Pete. I couldn't keep up with all the changes, but she just laughed.

"These days, I use and abuse them. It's the only way to keep 'em interested. Then I throw them away when I've had enough. That doesn't take me long - unless they treat me the way I want, they're gone!" she told me. She laughed even harder when I looked horrified.

"Be careful with Daz," she advised. "He seems to be a bit of a lady's man. I wouldn't trust him with ya' heart!"

Of course, I agreed with her to keep the peace, but it was way too late for that. I was in love! Daz had understood when I had told him of the attack, and that I wasn't ready for any physical intimacy. He was gentle and undemanding, cuddling and kissing with my feelings foremost in his mind.

Several weeks into the relationship we drove out to the lookout over the town and parked, looking at the view of the lights.

He slipped an arm around my shoulders and pulled me towards him. I'm sure he felt me stiffen, because he nuzzled into my neck and whispered that everything was OK. His other hand slid down to brush my breast, then cupped it as he kissed me. I pushed him away.

"Don't, Daz!"

"Aw, come on, love. I won't hurt you."

"Really, I can't. I'm scared!" I implored, looking into his brown eyes and sighed.

"It's ok - we'll be careful. It's about time you got over your uncertainty, and we took the next step in our relationship. You'd let me, if you loved me."

It was all said quietly, as he caressed my body with roving hands, and his mouth nibbled my lips as he spoke. The words entered my mouth and set my heart aflutter. I trusted him. I loved him. I was torn. I was frightened. I didn't feel ready but if I didn't give in, I might lose him.

I leaned back, and he moved over the top of me. His hand moved under my skirt and up my thigh. All the time his kisses were searing my mind into mush. I felt his fingers touch my knickers and move the material aside. I tried to stop him, but he kept murmuring.

"It's OK, honey. I love you. I'll be careful. It won't hurt." He stopped and took a breath, looking at me with eyes clouded with lust. "Oh my God, you're so wet!" he breathed, bending to kiss my breast as he pushed me further down onto the car seat. His fingers found my core, and I heard myself moan. I tried to push him away, but he didn't stop.

I held my breath and tried to move but the door was in the way, and my head was bent at an uncomfortable angle.

"Don't ... Please stop."

He didn't seem to hear. He pushed my legs apart with no notice of my struggles. One of my feet hit the steering wheel and the other slid over the top of the seat, dangling into the back. A shoe slipped off and fell. How and when I'd got into that position, I don't know. He pulled at my panties and I heard the material tear. I felt cool air on my intimate parts. I half protested, but his kisses and hands were driving me crazy. Then he opened his fly and released his hardened member. I closed my eyes and felt a rubbing of flesh on flesh on my most private area.

In the heat of the moment, I suddenly felt a stretching and filling of my nether regions, and realized he had entered me, and was pumping his body so hard, that my head was hitting the passenger side door and the window winder, bruising me. There was no way this could stop now.

Eventually, his body gave an almighty push and he stopped.

""Oh Clare," he breathed. That was wonderful!" He straightened his trousers, put my legs together and turned away.

I felt a gush of liquid on my skirt - I had no idea where my knickers were. Somehow they were gone. I tried to catch my breath. Was that it? Was that what sex was all about?

Well it hadn't done much for me. I felt used and sort of dirty, but when I looked at Daz, he was smiling.

"Thanks, hon. I always wanted to do that with you. That was great!" he said, before he started the car. "I'll take you home now."

When we got back to the flat, he leant over, gave me a quick kiss on my cheek, reached across me and pushed open the passenger door.

"See ya', honey," he oozed charm. "Great night! We'll do it again soon," I opened the door and got out. My knickers fell out onto the road. I clasped my skirt around me and bent to pick up my panties, as Daz roared off down the street. I let myself into my home, a little dazed, but still over the moon that Daz was my boyfriend and that he'd taken my virginity. It wasn't nearly as bad as I had been led to believe. I felt like shouting it from some mountain top or other. "I'm a Woman, now! He. Loves. Me." I hugged the wonder of it to myself. I wondered if it was always so uncomfortable for the woman, but Daz had seemed so pleased that I shook away the doubts.

The next day, as per my usual routine, I phoned Steve to let him know I had been out with Daz again, and that I was all right. Some sense told me not to mention my loss of virginity, but I did say that our relationship was getting serious.

"I'll always be your friend but be careful. Your boyfriend may not like the fact that you are friends with another male," he said.

When I protested he added, "I'll step back for a while. Let me know if you need me, but concentrate on yourself, and keep your friendship with Amy strong."

I tried desperately to convince him that it would be fine, but after a few minutes, I knew he was right.

I rang Amy.

Over that last few weeks, our friendship had got back to almost what it had been before her mother had left, and my attack had caused such a rift. I gushed with excitement about the fact that Daz had made love to me.

"Did you use any protection?" she asked after I finished telling her about the date.

That stopped me in my tracks.

"Um, no!"

"You'd better check to see if you're pregnant, and take 'the morning after' pill!" she advised.

The rest of the day, I worried. I was too embarrassed to go to the chemist and ask for the test kit, or the pill. Should I tell my parents? I should tell Daz, too, shouldn't I?

Daz had only been over to see me once, and we'd ended up in bed that night, too. He was aroused instantly we walked into the bedroom. We frantically tore at our clothes until we were naked, and then he entered me before I could even kiss him. It was over quickly and he was up, dressed and gone before an hour had passed. Again, we hadn't used any protection. I didn't feel as if I'd flown to the moon, or anything similar, but at least the bed had been soft, and when I was pinned to the bed, I didn't get bruised.

After a couple of weeks, my monthlies hadn't arrived, and I was convinced that I was pregnant.

I rang my mother.

"Are your breasts tender?" she asked, after she had finished telling me how disappointed she was that I had let this happen. When I answered yes, she told me to let Daz know, and that we should start planning the wedding.

Even though attitudes were changing, and many women now had children as single parents, my parents were definitely old-school.

"My grandchild is not growing up being ashamed of his birth," my mother said. "You'll have to get married."

I tried to resist, but Mum was insistent.

I rang Daz.

"Oh shit!"

I could hear the panic in his voice. Apparently his parents weren't pleased with the situation either, but were also old-fashioned and agreed with my parents. The wedding was on. Daz wasn't happy at the rush.

I knew how he felt, but within three weeks, we were in front of a marriage celebrant at the local courthouse, and we were husband and wife.

***

Even though the marriage had been unforeseen and rather hurried, I was still so much in love with Daz, that he could do no wrong. He moved into the flat with me, and we talked about getting a larger place for when the baby arrived.

Every night, Daz would roll me over onto my back and take me. The sex was part of my duty, so I did what was expected, sighing and gasping at the moments I thought I should. Daz didn't try to get me ready for the act, and it often hurt and I was unresponsive, but he seemed to enjoy it, so I never denied him.

Our life fell into a dull routine. I had given up my university course, and he had taken on a promotion at Coles retail store so that he got more money. I couldn't find a job as I expected to only work for a short while before I would have to give it up to be a full time mother.

Then one day, after only three weeks of married life, I began to bleed.

I immediately made an appointment with the doctor, scared that I was losing the baby.

The examination that I had to undergo was difficult for me, but afterwards, the doctor told me that I had not been pregnant, and this was merely the start of a late period.

I didn't know what to do.

When I told Daz that evening, he was so angry, that I became frightened.

"How dare you!" he shouted. "Didn't you go to the doctor and check before you tricked me into this sham of a marriage?"

I shook my head.

"I was too embarrassed!" I looked at the floor and kept my voice soft.

"Damn you! You fucking bitch!" he wheeled around and stormed out of the flat, slamming the door and leaving me standing in the middle of the room, tears spilling down my cheeks. Where he went I had no idea.

He didn't come home all night, and I cried myself to sleep. When he turned up the next morning, smelling of stale beer and looking as if he'd been lying in the gutter somewhere, I didn't say a word.

I placed a coffee and a bowl of cereal in front of him.

He didn't look at me, but grabbed the bowl and drank the coffee. When he finished eating, he got up, had a shower and went to work. Not a word had been spoken.

That night, the tension was palpable. When it came time for bed, I crept into the bedroom and slipped under the covers and pulled the blankets up to my chin.

Daz came in and yanked the sheets off. I tried to grab them and pull them back, but Daz threw the bed clothes on the floor and ripped my nightdress up to my navel. The protection I was wearing was unceremoniously tugged away, and blood pooled beneath my body. Daz took no notice, and began to push his fingers into me. Sex that night was rough and punishing. When I cried out, he merely pushed harder and faster. When he had finished, he turned over and went to sleep. I lay still, my body aching and bruised, blood of my period oozing and mixing with the blood from a tear in my perineum. I stared at the ceiling, not daring to move, for hours, wondering what I had let myself in for.

I crawled out of bed about five in the morning, careful not to disturb Daz. The sheets were soiled and my nightdress ruined. I sneaked out to the bathroom, washed myself then threw the nightie away.

By the time Daz was awake, I was dressed and drinking a morning cup of coffee. I stood, too sore to sit, looking out of the window. I don't even know what I was staring at.

Daz sidled into the kitchen and put his arms around me.

"I'm so sorry I hurt you last night. I was just angry."

He nuzzled my neck and smiled sheepishly. I melted and smiled back weakly, as a sudden sheen of tears washed across my vision.

Daz turned me to face him and kissed my forehead.

"So sorry, my love. I promise it won't happen again."

I nodded. My voice was choked with my love for him. This was understandable, and everything would be better when my body healed.

"It's ok," I mumbled, putting my cup of coffee on the sink and putting my arms around him.

"That's my girl!" he smiled, kissing me lightly on the cheek as he grabbed his jacket and headed off to work. I didn't see the smirk on his face as the tears blurred my vision. I was so relieved that he had forgiven me.

I knew what had happened was my fault, and I forgave his anger and his punishment. I resolved to be a good wife from now on, never complaining and making sure he was always happy.

When I rang Amy the next day to organize where to meet for our shopping spree, I told her I had lost the baby. I never mentioned the argument that had followed, or the hurtful sex that had occurred.

I had my pride.

To the outside world, our marriage was fine. The bruises where Daz had bitten my breasts and the soreness in my vagina from his violent thrusts I kept to myself. When Daz had pushed through the blood of my period and the way he had dragged my legs apart until I thought I would split and used me as if I was a package to be torn apart and tossed aside was not a subject up for discussion.

Besides, the quicker I got pregnant properly, the better things would be.

For the next few weeks, Daz was penitent and romantic, often bringing me flowers, and gently caressing me until I surrendered to his need for sex.

It didn't last.

Slowly the relationship began to deteriorate again. Daz took to staying out late night after night once more. If I questioned him, his temper would flare, and then the punishment for my lack of trust would be another night of rough sex. This began a slide into a vicious pattern until sex became his only way of communication, his way of dispelling his demons.

Every morning he would almost cry with his shame, apologising over and over. Telling me he loved me and didn't mean to hurt me. At times I couldn't walk I was so sore.

I would always forgive him. I loved him and my heart would believe that he would change even as my body ached.

Gradually, the sex got rougher and more often. Sometimes he needed sex every night, often more than once. He didn't seem satisfied until he had me crying with pain.

Afterwards I would get a respite for a week or two, and during that time, he would once again resort to romantic gestures – flowers, dinner out and picnics at the beach.

However, it never lasted, and the regime of terror would begin again with no reason that I ever understood.

One day he came home in the middle of the day, walked in and grabbed me.

He pushed me towards the kitchen table, threw me onto it on my back, yanked off my panties, ripping my dress as he rushed to enter me. He held me there, pulling my legs up onto his shoulders and lifting my buttocks high so he could get inside me deeply. I thought I was going to die. I shut my eyes and held on. The tip of his penis seemed to be riding up into my stomach, ramming against my innards at each violent thrust, and the pain was intense. Each movement was agony, and I clenched my teeth and forced myself to stay silent. He pulled out and semen washed all over my torn dress, up onto my face and into my mouth as he continued to jerk his member over me. I murmured, but didn't say a thing.

That was the first time he hit me.

"Whore!" he cursed, hitting me across the face, his hand sliding on his own juices. I flinched, trying to pull my torn skirt across my naked torso, without success. I lay on the table with my legs still open and my sex exposed to his sight. His eyes glanced down at my legs as they tried to find the floor so I could stand. He filled his mouth with spittle and spat at my vagina, still swollen and throbbing with pain. Then he turned and walked away, stomping out of the back door - leaving it open so the world could see my degradation.

It's ironic that I fell pregnant that day.

Several days later, the effects of another bout of punishing sex, caused me to bleed away the baby. I cried bitter tears. I had so hoped to be pregnant and back in Daz's good books. In my mind, struggling with Daz's change of attitude, a child would have fixed everything.

I never told him that I lost that baby. I was still trying to come to terms with the situation that was occurring. If he was going elsewhere for sex, it certainly hadn't stopped him from coming home and demanding his rights every night. Eventually it became every day as well, sometimes twice or more, morning, noon and night. He'd wake me in the middle of the night, and take more, never gentle, always rough sometimes cruel. He expected me to take him in my mouth, holding my head as he pumped and I gagged. He turned me on to my stomach and used my back passage for his penis while his fingers and sometimes fist, jammed into my vagina. Sometimes he tried the reverse. When I tried to stop him, he got more and more violent until I was too scared to say anything.

When I cried, he hit me. When I yelled at him to leave me alone, he hit me for answering him back. When I stayed silent and accepted the punishment, he hit me for not saying anything. It didn't matter what I did, I could not win. He hit me, sometimes, just for his own pleasure. He enjoyed looking at the pain in my eyes. One day he tied my hands behind my back with the electric kettle cable and masturbating into my face, holding my face with his other hand so I couldn't look away. It became a regular occurrence, and it became more and more cruel with sometimes knives or broken glass held at my throat. If I resisted he hit me until I could not stand, then fucked me as I lay on the floor. Often he would knock me down in the garden and grind dirt into my core, until I was red raw, then squirt the hose up me to make it easy for him to enter, If I cried with the pain, he merely did it again the next day.

Many times, I couldn't leave home, as two black eyes were hard to disguise. Bruises on my legs and arms quickly led to burst veins as they were continually hit, day after day. Once, he broke my arm as he twisted it behind my back and pushed me up against the shed's brick wall to reach his climax with anal sex.

And yet through all of this, I stayed and didn't mention it to a soul. If we went out, Daz was charming and caring. Holding my hand and hugging me in front of friends and family.

"You know," Amy said to me one day, "You were lucky you found Daz again. He's wonderful!"

I didn't deny it. How could I? I had no experience of marriage. My parents had been so in love it was sickening. Amy's parents had separated, so what happened behind closed doors was anybody's guess. I didn't have anything else to compare it to. I thought, in my innocence and misery that I had tricked him and therefore deserved what he did to me. I had been attacked by a gang of hoodlums, and broken by an angry husband. I must have done something extremely wrong. Or, I rationalized, that was what men were like and I didn't want anyone else to know what a poor wife to Daz I was that he should feel it necessary to act the way he did. Whenever we arrived home from any of the socializing we did, I would get more bruises, and he would be angrier. Then the sex was usually more aggressive, and lasted longer and longer as he strove to reach a climax. He was no longer so easily turned on, and made me suck his member for hours until there was a vestige of an erection, then place a band around the base so he could continue for hours until he came.

I fell pregnant once again.

This time I tried using the pregnancy to lessen the sex and the beatings. For a while that worked, but when I lost that baby as well, it started up all over again. He kept the punishment going. When he could no longer perform, he just beat me until I begged for mercy. When I begged, he swore and hit me more. I was a mess.

After twelve months of marriage and the trial that it had become, everything suddenly stopped.

No more anger.

No more fists to the face or limbs.

No more angry sex.

The bruises began to fade, and Daz, though silent and morose, stopped hitting me. He occasionally made love, still quick and savage, but even that became less and less often.

It always seems to me that we humans are a contrary lot.

Now I worried.

Had he found someone else? Had he lost his desire to fuck me to hell and back? Why?

And of course, I was pregnant once again.

This time I suffered. Morning sickness. Swollen ankles. Puffy face. Tender breasts. Stretch marks on my stomach as I quickly expanded into what I considered, a bloated mess. No longer attractive.

I worried. And I worried some more.

Daz began to come home later and later.

It started once a week, then twice a week, then every weekend. Once or twice he didn't come home at all overnight.

I was left alone. I was more terrified alone than I had been when Daz was at his nastiest.

How could I tell everyone that my marriage was a sham - a failure? To the outside world we looked as if we were a perfect couple. Daz always showed his charming side. He was kindness itself to everyone else, and pleasant to me. Only we knew it was a facade, and because there were now moments of peace in our marriage, and I had a baby to look forward to, I stayed. Daz was my one true love and, contrary to the violence that had marred the first twelve months of our marriage and had since faded, I still saw him through rose-coloured glasses.

I believed everything was fine when he told me the late nights and weekend absences were because of new shifts that he had been given.

In those moments when he was trying hard to get me to believe him, he became the man I had fallen in love with. Once more, the flowers appeared and he bought home gorgeous, sexy teddies and sex toys.

But when I wore them for him, I became a cowering mess, as he called me all the names he could think of.

"Whore!" he would shout, giving me another backhander.

"Slut," he would rage, spittle flying as he hit me with a whip until I sat in the corner of the room, trying to make myself small and an unlikely target.

"Cunt!" he would swear, as I lay bruised and bleeding once more. I tried to hide the clothes and not wear them - that didn't work either.

"Ungrateful Bitch," he would storm and then he'd punish me again.

Luckily, it didn't happened as much anymore, - but once again I fell pregnant. How my body still managed to create a child was beyond me. The love was long gone, and yet I kept thinking it was all my fault, and I was grateful for the pregnancy - hoping against hope that the baby would make us a family again.

Then I lost that child. Floating in a toilet bowl. Tearing away from my body with the same cruelness that had put it there in the first place. My only hope gone.

I lay in the bed, my whole life torn apart. My dream of a happy marriage and a stable family had disappeared and I had no chance of being a mother. I would never have a child to hold to my breast and love.

That is how I had got to this point.

This was my life.

Chapter 7.

I dragged myself through from day to day.

Still I told no-one of my despair.

Amy seemed to have disappeared again. Obviously she had found another new boyfriend. That occurred, for her, with monotonous regularity. Every time she was with another man, she fell off the radar, until the novelty had worn off, and she was ready to move onto someone new.

I had no-one to unburden my heart to.

I couldn't tell my parents.

I certainly couldn't complain to his family. They had all been disgusted when my pregnancy hadn't produced a child. His family had also accused me of tricking him into marriage. They seldom visited, and when they did they were openly hostile to me. Daz would parade me before them, showing my bruises and laughingly tell them I was so clumsy I was always falling over.

I couldn't tell Steve. Over the year I had lost contact with him, and I didn't know where he was. How I wished he was still my friend.

I was now so alone it hurt.

Somehow, we still managed to show a united front when we were out together. When Daz was home, it was like I was walking on eggshells.

We continued our pretence.

We were trapped in a convention that was years old. Neither of us was willing to admit to the outside world that we had failed. I continued to hope that he would change and love me as I wanted him to love me, but I was now almost certain he had found another woman.

He often came home smelling of booze and the mustiness of sex. I ignored it as he ignored me.

I was thankful for only two things.

The beatings had stopped and so had the violent sex. Occasionally he fondled me, and half-heartedly tried to perform, but either he no longer found me attractive, or he was already spent and exhausted from his time with the other woman.

When I murmured my love, he grunted, but never said a kind or gentle word to me. He merely turned away and went to sleep, as I stayed on my back, stiffly watching the ceiling, unable to sleep. I didn't have to do what was expected of me in the marriage any longer, and I missed the intimacy, even though it had been so violent.

I was lonely, unloved and depressed. I wished I was at least pregnant again and could look forward to a child to love, but that too eluded me.

I had to do something to save my sanity. So I decided to take up a hobby - outside of the home.

I joined an art group.

***

Every Wednesday afternoon at two o'clock, I made my way down to the local hall, arms full of brushes, canvas and paints. I sat for two hours with a group of elderly ladies all concentrating on creating a masterpiece.

"Hi, Clare," Betty trilled a greeting as I walked in the door. "How are you today?'

"Fine, thanks."

I smiled as I looked around the room. Six other ladies were setting up. There was Sonia, serious and studious; Helen with her penchant for wearing loud-coloured dresses; Tracy, red-haired, with a fiery temperament to match, and Judy of the wide smile and equally wide girth. Donna waved, a brush already dipped in paint and ready to make its first mark. Her long hair often got caught in the pots of colour, and she left the room with the ends a rainbow of shades. Grace was struggling with her easel, and let out a grunt that was supposed to welcome me. And there was, of course, Betty. That made up the eight of us all together.

By the time I was ready, the room was buzzing with muted conversation. Several of the women had surrounded Donna, and were commenting on her choice of subject.

Betty spoke to me in her usual lilting way.

"It's so lovely to have someone so young with us. You brighten up the whole place."

I grinned. If she only knew what my life was like and why I had joined, she would have been shocked.

"Thanks," I replied as I furrowed my brow. The darn bird I was painting was not coming along to my satisfaction. I absently added. "Now all we need is a male to enter these hallowed halls!"

"Oh no, dear." Betty clucked. "We're all here to get away from them!"

Judy laughed when she heard Betty.

"Talk for yourself," she snorted. "My Jack is one of the best!"

"Well, you're bloody lucky," countered Tracy. "They're not normally worth worrying about."

"Yeah," Donna got in to the conversation, turning away from her painting, waving her brush and scattering paint on the floor. "That's why I remained single."

Judy laughed. "You don't know what you're missing."

"Darn right!" Sonia glared at the rest of the group.

I sighed. This wasn't a conversation I wanted to join. I never said anything about Daz or my marriage – I discovered that I was unsure what to say and embarrassed in case I confessed my unhappiness. Even with all the snide comments about men, all the ladies were seemingly happy with their lot. Even the married girls laughed and joked about how horrible men were, but in the next breath were extolling their husband's good points. I could never think of anything good to say.

Silence returned as the paint flowed, and concentration reigned.

It was the same every week. The girls enjoyed the repartee, but the painting won out every time.

I enjoyed my release from the tension at home, and I looked forward to the absorbing couple of hours, that always seemed to be over far too soon.

One afternoon, I discovered I had left my gesso behind for preparing my canvas. I decided, as it was a beautiful day, to walk the few blocks back home to get it. I had nothing to carry, and, as it was only a short walk, I told the girls I would be back in half an hour.

It had been a long time since I could honestly say that I was at peace with the world. Daz and I had reached a point in our relationship that was fairly monotonous, but at least it was violence free. I knew there was little love left on both of our sides, but it no longer worried me. I walked along the street and enjoyed the warmth of the day, the slight breeze ruffling my hair, and the sun sifting through the leaves on the roadside trees. The gardens I passed were beautiful, and the only hiccup was the occasional dog that barked as I ambled by.

When I arrived at the flat I looked in my handbag to find the key, but as I stood there I realized that Daz's car was in the driveway. I tried the door, and it opened. I heard a muted conversation, and was elated to hear Amy's voice. We hadn't seen each other for a little while, although we often met for a quick cuppa and a chat once a week. I was due to see her tomorrow, and thought she must have come around to see me, not realizing I would not be home. What luck that Daz had decided to come home early.

I raced inside and looked around. No-one was in the lounge or kitchen area.

I heard a giggle, and followed the sound into the bedroom.

Amy was atop Daz, riding him for all she was worth. Daz's hands were tied to the bed-head with nylon stockings, and she wielded a whip playfully as she moved up and down. Daz's eyes were closed, and his face glowed with rapture as Amy giggled again.

"Ooh, Daz," she breathed. "You are such a naughty boy!"

Neither of them had heard me arrive, and I was so shocked that I froze and watched them with a horrifying fascination.

Whether it was the sudden gasp that I took, or the feeling that they were being watched I don't know, but suddenly Amy stopped, turned and looked at me. Her breasts continued to bounce slightly as she began to smile. Daz had obviously lost all arousal, because she lifted one of her legs and slipped off of him, leaving him naked and vulnerable. He tried to cover himself, but had forgotten the ties at his hands. He moaned.

Amy moved towards me.

I still hadn't moved.

She adjusted the leather top that was merely straps that showed her erect and moist nipples and threw the whip to land on Daz's flaccid penis. Her half-gloves showed bright red nail polish on each long fingernail and she laughed, holding them up, tossing her hair around and pretended to claw the air.

"Rraooar!" She licked her lips. "Come on Kitten - join in. I'm sure Daz would love to see you being whipped in front of him. I have another much more effective weapon that I would use on you - they used to call them cat-o-nine tails."

I backed away, not able to speak from the anguish that flowed through my body.

Daz groaned again. I wondered why he was not saying anything, but when I got up the courage to look at him, he was not only tied to the bed by feet and hands, but gagged as well.

Amy turned back and bent over him and kissed his genitals as he lay there helpless. His penis once more began to quiver and become erect. She smiled and licked his member until it stood straight and hard.

I turned and fled from the room. Tears were streaming down my face, but I hadn't noticed. To think my husband and my best friend could do this to me.

As I left, Amy laughed and I heard her say.

"Now! Gorgeous! Where were we? You haven't had your money's worth yet. I'll get another whip and turn you over, so I can use it and the handle in all sorts of wonderful ways. Won't it be fun when I hurt you again?"

I escaped the flat and ran.

***

When I ran out of breath I was at the local park. I sat on the same park bench where I had often sat and contemplated my life. I took some deep breaths to control myself.

Was I really that upset? Daz wasn't my problem. I was actually more hurt by Amy.

How long had this affair been going on?

I thought about it, and suddenly the end of the violence for me seemed to be a sign of the beginning. That would make sense.

Suddenly, I felt like laughing.

How ironic!

He was now the one being hurt. The things he put me through must have made him unable to have sex unless there was pain and violence.

Oh, but fate was wonderful. I stood up and strength flowed through me. I was actually looking forward to going home, to see how he would react now that I had caught him with Amy. Whether I would ever be friends with Amy, however, was another thing altogether.

I arrived home later that evening to a silent house.

I set about making dinner. Now, I would be able to place the dinner in front of him without fear. I knew his secret, and it gave me more power than I'd ever felt before.

I waited.

When he finally sneaked in the back door, I was ready. I had eaten my food, and left his on the table, now cold and unappetizing.

He looked at me with intense hate, and I wondered if he would strike out at me again. He sat at the table in silence, ate the meal then got up and walked out of the room, and went to bed.

It was the pattern of our days from then onwards.

The marriage could sink no lower. The uselessness of each day, threw me into depression, and I didn't know where to turn.

I often went to the park. I didn't return to the art group, and I wondered idly if they had tried to find out what had happened when I didn't return that fateful day.

Sometimes I would just sit on that same bench and stare into space. I liked to call it meditating, but really I was just absent.

When the weather was cold, overcast and rainy, I suffered the most, but I still went to the park to escape the dreariness of my existence.

The ground was soft and cold. Sometimes, if I sat on the grass, the dampness would seep into my clothes; I thought it might ooze into my soul.

So many memories.

Some I didn't want to remember.

Nothing changed, until the day the phone rang and it was Amy.

"Don't hang up," She implored. "I've rung to apologize."

I sneered into the handset as if she could see my disgust. "Saying sorry doesn't help. I don't want to talk to you."

As I moved to cut her voice off and have the satisfaction of slamming the phone down on her, I heard "He paid me to do it!"

It stopped the action, but not the hurt and my distrust.

"Don't lie to me!" I snarled and was glad she couldn't see the tears in my eyes.

"Really, Clare. It was all an act! He paid me - he's been paying me for months. It's how I make my money, these days."

I snorted.

"Why didn't you tell me this weeks ago?" I don't know why I kept the conversation going. I didn't want to see or hear Amy ever again.

"I couldn't!"

"Why not? - No, don't answer that - I don't want to know. I don't ever want to see you again!" This time I hung up. It mightn't have been a crash of the phone and a dramatic scene, but it was done, and it helped me feel better.

I began to plan.

I had to leave.

This marriage was going nowhere and I was suffering more than before. When he was beating me I was too scared to go, frightened he would search me out and hurt me more, even kill me. Now I had the upper hand, but I also knew I was no longer afraid to go.

But where could I go? I wasn't going to go back home. I was too old and scarred to face my parents. I had to find a sanctuary.

There were places to go that hid you and supported you, a refuge from the violence, but they were few and far between, and besides they were bursting at the seams with women that had become victims. I wasn't going to do that. I wasn't going to admit to anyone else that I was unable to look after myself. I had to find somewhere else to live.

Chapter 8.

The first thing I did was return to the art group.

When I arrived, the girls clamoured around me.

"We've missed you!" Betty clasped my hand and smiled.

"Where have you been?"

"Are you OK?"

"It's been ages,"

"Sit down and tell us what you've been doing?"

Everyone spoke at once and I was blown away by the bombardment of questions. I waved them away and took a breath so deep I got tingles!

"Whoa! One at a time! Pleeeease!"

Tracy laughed.

"Get her a cuppa, someone - I think we're in for a long story!"

"No, I'm fine." I shook my head and started to unpack my paints. "I'm just having a mid-life crisis!!"

I laughed to show I was joking.

Donna patted me on the arm. "Now don't be silly!" she said. "You're not old enough for that."

I knew I could never tell them about my problems, I couldn't ask for advice or help. I had intended to when I first arrived, but I was too mortified to open my wounds for them.

So I lied. An outright, unashamed lie!

"Sorry, girls. Went away for a while, then was sick when I came back. I'm right now, though."

"But you never returned to pick up your canvas when you went home for the gesso. We were worried."

"Yeah - about that..." I gritted my teeth and hoped they would believe my next comment. "Um - when I got home, my husband whisked me away on a surprise trip!" Definitely, I thought - it was a BIG surprise!

And he'd been the one on the trip - he'd fallen, made a blunder and - I think Amy would have called it - gone around the world.

The girls all started up again.

"So lucky!"

"Wow, what a surprise!"

"Lucky you."

"Where'd you go?"

"Did you have a good time?"

I tried to smile, accept their compliments and questions, but it was way too much for me to handle. Perhaps I was a bit ungrateful, and a little tactless. Perhaps I could have been more gracious and understanding, but I'd had enough.

"Well, I'm back now. Let's paint!"

The hilarity died down, and we each went back to our easels. The next hour passed with little sound as we all concentrated on the tasks in front of us. By the time the session had finished, my head was throbbing and I was ready to go home, even though home had never represented anything safe. At least it would be quiet and I could rest and hopefully get rid of the headache. Daz wasn't likely to be home for hours, and when he arrived he and I no longer interacted on any level anyway.

***

I soon discovered that making a decision to leave, and actually doing it, were two different things.

Day after day I made excuse after excuse. I spoke to no-one in my family, I didn't contact Amy, and I sunk into a despondency that was difficult to rise above. Every few days I ventured down to the real estate agent to enquire about places to rent, but there was never anything available that I would have been able to afford.

Somehow, I had to get some money together, but Daz reluctantly gave me such a small amount for food, and I had no job of my own to earn any.

How was I going to get away? Was it even worth it?

I still went to the art group intermittently and on one of my visits, Donna mentioned a small cabin in the local caravan park. She sat at the easel with brush poised in the air, closed her eyes and sighed.

"Oh! What I would give to go to the beach in a cabin for a week and just paint!"

Sonia grinned.

"You and me both!" she said, then added. "The local caravan park rents them out at a ridiculously cheap rate, and you don't need a bond to stay in them."

I listened intently, hoping they would tell me more. It sounded like the answer to my prayers.

"Yeah, I know." Donna's brush and eyes went back to her art work. "But it's not the same as bein' at the beach."

The conversation flagged, but it had given me an idea.

When I got home, I took out the phone book and began to look for caravan parks in the local area, but not too close. I wanted somewhere safe where I wouldn't easily be found. There wasn't much choice. However I found an advertisement for one a couple of suburbs away.

I paced around the room for several minutes, trying to get up the courage to ring them.

What could I say? Would they know I was running away from my life? Would they hear the tremor in my voice? Perhaps I shouldn't do this? I put the phone book down and made myself a cup of tea. I couldn't do this. It was too difficult.

If Daz found out my plans would he go back to punishing me, or would he be relieved and let me go? I daren't think about it. I was so scared again.

Several days ago he had lashed out and given me a black eye. He didn't apologize, just walked away. The violence was beginning again. Maybe Amy had stopped her service. Perhaps Daz didn't have the money to pay her anymore. I had heard his shifts had been cut at the supermarket because he had often not arrived to do his job, and he was now in danger of being fired.

That would mean he would be home and drunk more often. It wasn't a pleasant thought to have. I knew that would mean more suffering for me.

Damn!

I picked up the phone again and dialled the number. It rang several times, and my hand wavered, ready to put down the phone.

"Yes? Can I help you?"

I had to answer.

***

Two weeks later, Daz came home early one afternoon. He looked livid.

"Your bitch of a girlfriend has left the area."

This did not re-assure me in the slightest. This could mean several things. Maybe he had been dumped by Amy. Maybe she had decided not to continue her 'business', or maybe her mother had finally informed her of her whereabouts, and Amy had decided to go to her. There were so many possibilities. It made Daz's increasing violence at home more understandable, and all the questions running around in my head had been partially answered.

The other thing that concerned me was that now Daz had no outlet for his fantasies and cruelties, I would become his punching bag more and more, just as I had suspected.

I wasn't wrong.

That night he harassed me once again, giving me a cut lip with a vicious back-hander when I tried to stand up and be strong. Once Daz made up his mind to fuck me, I hadn't the physical strength to resist. I ended up on the floor, bruised and hurting, once again divested of my dignity.

It was the proverbial straw that broke the camel's back. I knew I had to make a decision and leave as soon as I possibly could, even though I was terrified that he would find me if I ran.

The next morning, as soon as Daz left for work, I packed a bag with a jumble of clothes. I really had no idea what I had taken as the tears blurred the outlines, and the panic, which had my heart racing and my hands clammy with sweat, caused me to just grab and run.

The only means of escape was by bus.

I boarded a bus to the city, got off halfway, and re-boarded a bus to the suburb where the caravan park was situated. Hopefully, if Daz asked anyone if they had seen me, someone would be able to send him to the city on a wild goose chase.

I walked into the park with a smile and a false confidence, asking to rent one of the cabins for a fortnight. That used most of the money I had saved, so it meant that I would have to find a job quickly.

No questions were asked, and I was soon sitting on a single bed in a small room with my suitcase at my feet, my head held by shaking hands, with my elbows balanced on wobbly knees.

The bed cover was worn and slightly threadbare, although I had no doubt that it was clean. There was a television opposite, perched on a shelf. Next to it was a built-in single wardrobe. A small dingy kitchen and a tiny bathroom with a toilet completed the cabin. The place smelled of stale smoke, and the walls were a drab grey. This was going to be my home for the foreseeable future. It felt like a prison. I almost got up to go back home. The bruises on my arms and legs as well as my dignity forced me to stay seated.

I sat and cried.

What had I done?

Chapter 9.

For the first three days, I stayed on the bed and stared blankly at the walls. Occasionally I stumbled to the kitchen and made myself a drink or a snack. I turned on the television and sat and watched, not understanding or caring what I watched.

Most of the time I slept. My brain was a morass of jumbled thoughts. I had no idea what to do or where to turn. I wallowed in my own misery, awash with more doubts and different fears. Sometimes I sat and cried. I couldn't believe that I had walked away from my marriage, and I was in constant fear that Daz, or maybe the police, would arrive and drag me home.

Instead of feeling free, I continually missed my flat, and Daz.

It didn't make sense.

Finally, I awoke and realised that this could not continue. I needed to break out of the grip of depression and find a job. I had no intention of crawling back to my marriage, as I knew I would probably not survive - either the humiliations or the beatings I was sure to get.

I searched through the pitiful supply of clothes that I'd managed to stuff into the suitcase, got up on trembling legs and went to the bathroom.

I stood under the dribble of tepid water from the shower until I began to feel human again. I felt as grey and listless as my surroundings.

When I got out of the shower, I stood and surveyed myself in the pock-marked mirror. My hair was an insipid colour that could do with some highlights. My face showed the signs of the crying I'd done, with puffiness around each soulless eye. The lines beside my mouth were deep and permanent from months of never smiling.

I dressed slowly and unhappily. I hadn't got a fashionable bone in my body, and Daz had never given me enough money to be able to buy clothes. The only time he bought me a dress was when we had to go out together and he picked what I would wear. The clothes I had thrown into my bag in such a rush were old and faded. Now they simply hung on my thin body. I didn't know if I dared to show myself to the world, yet I had to. I didn't have enough money for food to eat, let alone pay for the privilege of staying in this drab and confining cabin. My only advantage was that here, in this suburb, I could be anonymous.

I stood in the middle of the room and took several deep breaths. I had escaped from Daz - that had taken courage. I had found this place to live. Now I needed to draw on that courage. I clenched my fists, lifted my chin and opened the door to the rest of my life.

***

The first thing I had to do was find a job and after the endless months of being beaten and told how stupid I was, I was sure no-one would consider me.

I felt as if there were letters painted on my forehead in bright red. 'I AM USELESS! DON'T HIRE ME. I AM WORTHLESS'. My self-esteem was almost at rock bottom.

But I kept walking, out of the caravan park and down to the local shopping centre.

I walked into one shop after the other, asking, in a voice that even to me sounded hushed and frightened, if they needed a worker.

I didn't go to the big store in case Daz would look for me there. I didn't enquire at the hotels for the same reason.

After an hour, I returned to my cabin - deluded and more depressed than before. There was no light at the end of the tunnel, no job, no hope.

My thoughts were turning inwards more and more. I knew I had no more time. I felt so useless, and I considered finishing it all together.

No-one would care. No-one would miss me.

My parents no longer communicated with me. Daz and his family would be happy I was gone. Amy had disappeared and I had no idea where Steve was.

I sat and cried.

Where the tears came from was beyond my comprehension. I thought I had no more liquid to give, but it was all I seemed capable of doing.

In the end, I discovered I was even too scared to take my own life. That realization was demoralizing, but it jerked me into the now; struck some sort of nerve inside my shattered esteem. This could not go on. I had to do something.

Not long afterwards, with my last few cents, I walked to the local shop, knowing I could only afford some food to last me one more day. I was desperate. I needed a job.

"Hello, Clare." A chirpy voice said behind me. "Fancy seeing you here."

I turned into a pair of opened arms and was hugged to an ample bosom.

Betty just stood and held me. I stiffened – embarrassed that I had been found and terrified that she would hate me now if she found out what I had done.

"My God, girl. You look terrible! What an earth has happened?" I knew I had become thin, and the dress I had on, faded and threadbare, only accentuated the boniness of my body.

As I continued to look down at the pavement, my hair in oily strands falling forward and hiding my face, Betty gently put her hand on my shoulders, turned me around and guided me to the café next to the shop.

I melted onto the seat, and stared at the table in front of me, too ashamed to look up into her friendly face.

Betty sat down.

"What's happened?" She asked again, sounding so concerned that I could feel the tears sting behind my eyes.

"Nothing," I mumbled. I couldn't tell her. I was still trying to deny the wretchedness of my life to myself – how could I admit it to another?

But Betty was patient.

She disappeared and I thought about escaping. Before I'd gathered the strength and the energy to move, she was back. A plate of chips, a hamburger and a cup of coffee were put in front of me.

I looked up and Betty smiled.

"Eat up," she said. "You look as if you need it!"

The kindness undid me. I sniffed back the tears and wolfed down the chips, eating the hamburger as if I hadn't had a good meal for months. That wasn't far from the truth.

As I drank the coffee, my body warmed for the first time in what felt like years. I had forgotten the feeling of true friendship and the terror of my marriage has made me suspicious and protective of my feelings. Now Betty had begun to crack the shell I had woven around me– all with a meal, a coffee and her concern.

It didn't take long for Betty to learn I had nowhere to go and nothing in my purse. She didn't hesitate.

"Let's go and get the rest of your stuff from the caravan. You're coming home with me."

She bundled me into her car, talking all the time, telling me her husband had been looking forward to meeting me. When she got to the caravan park, she took no notice of my weak protestations, collected my few possessions and gave the park management the information that I was leaving.

My head was spinning, partly, I suspected, from dizziness caused by a strong cup of coffee and the first decent food I'd had for weeks – and partly from the sudden change in my circumstances and the brisk management from Betty, who I'd always considered a woman with not much compassion or, in fact, to my embarrassment and shame, intelligence.

Her husband, Tony, was a cheerful, rotund sort of man, who obviously adored his wife. He welcomed me into their home with a breadth of good humour to match his girth.

I finally felt safe.

Chapter 10.

Betty and Tony showered me with a love I had never experienced before. Unselfish and uncomplaining, they continued to look after me, until my mind and body began to heal.

Over the intervening weeks, I slowly let them know what had happened. It took courage, and I could only bear to tell them a little each time, before my mind would shut down and refuse to continue They never pushed, they never judged, they just gave me room to become myself again.

The home was warm and the gardens serene. I took to sitting outside and letting the peace of Nature flow through my veins. Betty would sometimes sit with me. We would sip our drinks in companionable silence. Tony often joined us, but he couldn't sit still. The weeds annoyed him and he was soon down on his knees, plucking them from his rose garden.

I was amazed when I started to help him. It had been a gradual process, but I was regaining my desire to do something constructive, and I realised, with a quiet inward smile, I had begun to trust again. The trust, like me, was still fragile, but it was a start. I began to see a glimmer of hope.

One day, passing a mirror, I was pleased I could stop and look at myself. It had been a long time since I had been courageous enough to look at my face. I stood there for several minutes, just looking.

My hair, no longer lank and oily, had bounce and lustre. My cheeks were full and pink, not pale and unhealthy. My lips were full and lush, instead of bruised and swollen. They weren't compressed into a hard thin line of worry, and my face had lost the stress and wrinkles that had made me look years older.

I took a step closer.

My eyes were clear, the bags of tiredness had disappeared and the lines on my forehead had begun to smooth out.

I was able to smile.

"If you could only see me now, Daz!"

Had I said that out aloud?

My face immediately frowned and the lines re-appeared! I shuddered inwardly, and my fear returned.

I walked away, stunned how quickly I had sunk back into my old persona. I was still not ready to face the world.

***

Several weeks later I was helping Tony in the vegetable patch. Betty had gone to the painting class alone, as she had yet to convince me to return there.

"Um," Tony stopped and sat back on his haunches. "I ... He sighed.

I looked up from planting the lettuce seedlings. Spring had come, and the day was balmy. It was the quintessential day – bees humming, birds singing – the leaves of the grevilleas rustling in the slight breeze – a Willy wagtail chirruping and chiacking nearby.

"Yes?" I said, waiting for him to get his thoughts together.

Tony shook his head.

"Forget it."

He went back to adding the tomato seedlings to his side of the bed.

"Come on, Tony. Something's bothering you. Out with it."

I could see he was uncomfortable. I decided to say something that had been rattling around in my brain for the last week or so.

"You know, Tony – I've been thinking." I stopped. I didn't know how to say what I wanted to say either. These two people had been so good to me and I appreciated it so much. I didn't want to hurt them.

I continued. "I really should start getting out. I need to look for a job."

He smiled.

"That's what I was wanting to say, but I didn't want you to think we were trying to push you away."

I got up, brushed the dirt off my hands and knees, went around to him and gave him a hug.

"I would never think that – you have both been so wonderful to me – but it is time I thought of standing on my own two feet again. Perhaps I can even go back to do some study later."

He nodded, unable to say much, as his emotions were plain to see. He was such a lovely man. I'd forgotten that there were such decent males in the world.

By the time Betty arrived back from the painting class, I had showered and changed into a simple skirt and blouse.

I was ready to re-start my life.

Chapter 11.

Getting dressed in my new uniform was unusually exciting for me. I was scared as well. Starting a new job was something I had never had to do before.

I had been ecstatic when I had landed a job that first day. I was going to be a check-out chick in the local Coles store and I couldn't be happier or more proud of myself.

I hurried in to the kitchen to down a cup of coffee to settle my nerves. Betty smiled.

"Woohoo!" she sang. "Don't you look smart!"

I twirled around, my arms out and the grin on my face nearly splitting it in two. I went over to her and enveloped her in the biggest hug I could manage. Betty was sitting on the breakfast stool, with a steaming cup of coffee in her hands. She held the cup away from herself in trembling hands.

"I'm so happy!" I said. "I'm not anything like the girl you rescued just a few short months ago – I can't thank you enough."

Betty laughed.

"Whoa – careful – you'll spill my coffee," she said, but her eyes moistened with unshed tears as she put the coffee down on the bench and hugged me back.

***

That first day at work was the best and the worst day of my new life. I was so nervous, and I made several mistakes. I spent times anxious and panicky, wondering if I would still have the job by the end of the day. I was so worried that I would be punished. All the old fears came rushing back. I must have looked like a cringing mouse, trying desperately to avoid a confrontation with the house cat!

The supervisor, Nell, was patient and understanding.

"We all have to have a 'first' day when we have a new job, Clare. Don't worry so much – you'll get the hang of it."

By five o'clock I was exhausted but elated. Somehow I had conquered the upsurge of fear and continued through the day. I stood at the front of the store at the end of my shift and felt like dancing.

I was a working girl.

I was no longer a frightened, beaten and downtrodden woman.

I felt free.

Tomorrow was going to be a better day and my life was only going to improve from there.

When I arrived back at Betty's and Tony's I was brimming with new-found confidence and happiness.

***

Later, when I came back down to earth, the rush I had felt became a deep flood of uncertainty. In my time with Betty and Tony I had managed to put Daz and my life with him to the back of my mind, but now I had ventured out into the world again, the self-hate and shame were making an appearance again. I lay in bed of a night, convincing myself that the staff at Coles could see my flaws; that they only smiled and were friendly because they *had* to, not because they meant it.

I got up the next morning, striving to keep up my facade; my anxieties hidden.

Over the next few days it was difficult, and I stumbled many times, but gradually, the smile on my face became easier to maintain, and the doubts once again shrunk into a small corner of my mind.

Gradually my self-esteem strengthened and my panic attacks lessened. Some days at the job went well and I felt as if my life was now on an even keel. I began to seriously consider the possibility that I should find my own home. When I was no longer terrified that Nell would fire me and the job seemed secure, finding a small inexpensive flat closer to my work sounded like a good idea. The biggest problem I faced was finding the courage to tell Betty and Tony.

One evening, after a delicious roast dinner, we were all sitting in the lounge, sated and satisfied. I broached the subject.

"Boy that was a great meal!" I leant back on the chair, patting my distended stomach while sighing dramatically. Contented murmurs were my only answer.

"It would be really nice to be able to have you come to my home for a meal like that," I continued dreamily.

Tony glanced over. Betty smiled and nodded her head slightly.

"Yes, dear. One day!"

"I think I'll start looking for a place this week," I added.

"Mm mm OK!"

But I could sense that they didn't really believe me.

***

It seemed appropriate somehow. Exactly one year to the day I had taken my life in my hands and walked away from my marriage, I burst into the kitchen after work. Betty was standing at the sink peeling potatoes. I presumed Tony was out in the garden.

"I found it!" I shouted, swinging Betty around with my excitement. She laughed, one hand holding a potato high, the other shedding a peel from the peeler as she turned.

"Settle, honey," she said as she staggered a little and put down the potato and peeler, then looked at me. There was a sparkle in her eyes, but she frowned slightly. "What have you found?"

"The perfect flat!" I gurgled, unable to keep a straight face.

"What?" Betty's smile disappeared.

"It's only small, but I love it!" I prattled on, not catching the disappointment oozing from Betty. "It's got a dinky bathroom, and there's two bedrooms, and a lounge, and the carpet on the floor is in good nick, and they've left the curtains up and there's even a ... kitchen ... table

..." I ground to a halt. Betty had sat down and was looking as if she was going to cry.

I walked over to her and bent down.

"What's wrong?" I asked.

She shook her head as if to shake off her feelings.

"Nothing!" she said, trying to smile.

"Gosh, Bet – I thought you'd be happy for me." I bit my bottom lip. "I'm sorry."

"Don't apologise," she answered. "I knew this day would come – just didn't expect it so soon!"

"But I told you I would be looking, and you didn't seem to mind."

"When?" She looked up, puzzled.

Before I could answer, Tony came into the room, going straight to his wife with concern on his face.

It took an hour and two more cups of coffee before I could convince my two rescuers that I wasn't leaving them because I was sick of their company.

"You're not ready!" Betty kept insisting.

"I know," I replied, "but I have to do this for my own good. I can't lean on you both forever."

"Yes you can!" Betty dabbed at her eyes with her lacy handkerchief.

Tony put his arm around her shoulders.

"You're going to have to let Clare go," he said, "even if you don't want to. She has to try to live alone. We can help her."

Betty brightened visibly.

"Ok!" her voice trembled, but she smiled at me. "We can help you with the move, the furnishings and we will always be here if you need us."

I grinned.

"You two are the best! I don't know what I would have done, or will do, without you."

I tried to put my arms around both of them and hug.

We all ended up in tears amid the laughter and love.

***

A week later I stood in my own flat, only ten minutes walk from work.

I had just waved goodbye to Betty and Tony and I was alone.

The lounge felt homely and warm. My sofa was a subtle shade of chocolate, and the accessories that Betty had added pinpointed stabs of colour. I sank down into its comfort, and wondered what I had done. The aroma of the lamb stew Betty had made wafted from the kitchen. Betty had filled the fridge with a week's worth of dinners and desserts even though I had tried to stop her. I was more appreciative than she would ever know.

My bed was made up with plenty of blankets, and the Manchester cupboard was filled with Betty's towels and sheets.

"I've got too many," she had said as she had bundled them into my arms.

I turned on the small TV and went back to the lounge, curling up and watched the news. I was already lonely, but I knew I had had to break my dependency on them, even if I really didn't want to. Betty and Tony had been more parents to me than my own, who had been disappointed in my decision to marry Daz. I had been amazed that they had been contrarily disappointed when the marriage had failed; blaming me as if it had been my fault. They hadn't spoken to me since I had telephoned them and told them I had moved in with Betty and Tony.

On my first day alone, I crawled into bed as soon as the sun sank. I thought about everything that had happened in the last few years – the elation of my love for Daz, the horror that my marriage had become, the decline into a depression of low self-esteem and self loathing and then the courage to take that first step to a new life. Finally, the strength I had gained with the love and support of Tony and Betty.

I felt a faint niggle of fear crawl along my body, but I turned my face into the pillow and ignored it. Surprisingly, I fell asleep immediately.

Chapter 12.

Work kept my mind from dwelling on my loneliness, but several times I had to ring Betty and she came over and calmed me as my anxiety attacks had returned.

"You should come back with us," she said over and over again.

I used all of my self-control to refuse. The weakness of my desire to agree to her suggestion was hard to overcome, but I knew I had to keep trying. When I had calmed, and she had left, I would sit under a blanket, cold and lonely. The television blared with Countdown and Molly Meldrum giving the pop stars their publicity, but I didn't really see or hear the music. I just needed the sound to fill my emptiness.

I often thought of Billy and the gang that had held me down and made me so vulnerable. I wondered if that incident had left me in a position to accept the violence of my marriage to Daz.

Then I thought of Steve. I had thought of him often during the 3 months since I had moved into the flat. I had allowed him into my thoughts even before I had left the safety and protection of Tony and Betty. In fact I had thought about him more than I had expected to.

I wished I hadn't lost contact and I hoped he thought of me, if not as often, at least sometimes.

It was with astonishment the next day, when Steve walked into the shop as if the Universe had answered my desire.

I must have looked shocked. He had a black eye and a raw red scratch down his cheek. He limped over to the checkout. I hadn't moved. My customer was also frozen in place, the scene stilled with anticipation.

Steve broke the spell.

"When you're free, I want to talk to you," he said to me, and he didn't sound happy.

I nodded. I began to tremble with fear. He looked ready to hit me, and, other than my father (who was distant and concerned only with work and my mother) and Tony (sweet, helpful man that he was), the only other male I had been close to had made me touchy and scared of any type of anger.

I went back to finishing the order of the customer in front of me, but my insides had turned to jelly with dread. I gave her change, not sure if I had got the amount correct, then left the checkout, spoke to my boss, and walked outside with my head high, hiding my anxiety.

I found Steve pacing the pavement outside.

He whirled around, grabbed me by the shoulders and looked deeply into my eyes.

"Why didn't you tell me?" He was almost yelling.

I shrunk back and looked at my feet. When would he hit me? Would he shake me until my teeth rattled? Should I run?

I began to tremble outwardly now. I blinked to stop the tears falling that had blurred my eyes and I tried to stop my knees from giving way and allowing my weakness to show.

I lifted my head.

Before I could fight back, I was clasped to his chest, arms holding me tight and I could feel that he was trembling as well.

"Oh, my God, Clare. How could you have been treated like that? The bastard!"

I frowned, and pushed him away. He looked at me and I could see pity in his eyes. I dredged up an anger I didn't know I was capable of.

"So you think it was my fault? Do you think I asked for this? Do you think I like being a failure? I hate you! I hate you! You are just like him."

I turned, tears now unchecked were running down my face, and ran, ran as fast as I could. I ran, without direction, without care. I heard him call my name, but I didn't stop.

I didn't stop until I reached Betty and Tony's. How I got there, I had no idea. Had I caught the bus? It was too far away from my work to have run all the way, although the blisters on my feet told me different. I stopped, trying to catch my breath. I walked through the gate, tears now gone. My eyes felt swollen and puffy, my insides twisted and raw with emotion and my lungs breaking as I still gulped for air after my desperate escape.

I found them in the garden.

Betty rushed over.

"What's happened?" she asked, fluffed and ready to protect me like a mother hen.

"I saw Steve," I cried. "He yelled at me and I ... then I lost my temper 'cos I was so frightened and I was awful to him ... and then I ran away." My voice hiccoughed and broke as I talked.

"Why? What did he do? What did he say?" Tony bristled with indignation.

"Nothing! Well, nothing very much!" I cried even more, tears of relief, tears of confusion, tears of the knowledge of my failure to be strong. "I don't know what he said!" I moaned, then looked at my two friends and said, very quietly, "Then he ... he hugged me!"

Betty looked at Tony – a furrow of wrinkles on both their foreheads.

"Hugged you?"

"He hugged me," I repeated, softer still, and confused.

"So ... why are you crying? Why are you here?"

I looked at them both, standing there, looking at me as if I'd lost my mind.

"I don't know," I confessed, wiping at my eyes, allowing the mascara to smear across my cheeks. Betty silently handed me her handkerchief and I took it, sobbing into it anew, rubbing my face, blackening the lace and cotton.

It was Tony who spoke next.

"Aren't you supposed to be at work?"

I gasped – I had asked Marge, the supervisor at the checkouts that day, for a ten minute break. I looked at my watch. Forty minutes had passed. I had to get back. I couldn't lose my job.

Tony hustled me into his car.

"Come on – I'll explain to your boss."

We got back in record time, and after he spoke to Marge, I was back at the checkout.

I had to make up the time, but I had kept my job.

***

When my shift ended, I was shattered. On top of the emotions that Steve's appearance had awoken, the extra hour packing shelves in lieu of the break I had taken completely finished me. My legs were aching from the running I had done and my head throbbed with pain. All I wanted was to drink a hot, sweet cup of tea and then collapse into bed.

I hoped Betty and Tony wouldn't decide to come over to my place in order to make sure I was all right. I'd told Tony that I would be all right and even though he had wanted me to go back to their place after my shift, I had managed to convince him to tell Betty not to worry. I had even put all thoughts of the encounter with Steve out of my mind, a talent I had acquired when my marriage had become too horrible to contemplate, so, when I gratefully finished work and walked outside, the last person I expected to see was Steve.

But there he was.

I stopped, ready to flee once again, but Steve stood there with his arms wide open and hands upturned.

"Clare, don't go ... please."

I didn't move. I couldn't. I think I moaned but I'm not sure.

He took a hesitant step forward, speaking softly and quickly as he did so.

"It's taken me so long to find you. Please talk to me."

I couldn't speak – there were so many thoughts going through my mind. Embarrassment as I remembered the way Steve had found me in the first place. Fear as the memory of the crowding around me when the gang had tried to rape me – the taking away of my innocence, the indignity of my uncovering, and the shame when I remembered I had allowed the violence that Daz had put me through. All I could see of the Steve in front of me, was the violence I had come to expect from males – the black eye and blood-encrusted scratch on his face only supporting the image I had of men. Perhaps he had become violent, too.

I stepped back, but Steve kept pleading and I swallowed down my panic, replacing it with anger.

"Stay away from me!" I yelled unaware that tears had begun to trickle down my cheeks once more.

Steve didn't move – his voice lowered and gentled.

"Shh. I promise I won't hurt you – I just want to talk."

"I don't believe you," but I felt my control wavering, as my voice broke, and my legs felt like jelly, threatening to fold under me and drop me to the pavement. I felt eyes upon me, an audience I didn't want or need. I looked around desperately for somewhere to sit. I needed to collapse into it so I didn't disgrace myself any more in front of everyone. I saw a seat a few steps away and frantically moved towards it, hoping against hope that I could reach it.

Steve stood still, watching, afraid to shatter the moment.

After a journey of what felt like a million miles, I reached the seat. My sight had become a blurred tunnel of vision. I couldn't hear anything but the blood pulsing through my head. The world had gone silent, and my body was shaking furiously, and there was no way I could control it.

I felt someone sit beside me and then arms pulled me into an embrace. A voice kept caressing me with soothing words. What the words were or who sat there, I had no idea. I was in the middle of a full blown panic attack.

***

I could feel myself calming down. I took deep breaths, and tried to remember the steps Betty had told me to use. I was alright. I was going to be fine. I kept repeating these thoughts over and over.

The arms still embraced me even though I must have struggled against them. The warmth and smell of the sweater that I was snuggling into felt familiar.

Gradually my surroundings began to coalesce into normal. I looked up. Steve looked back.

I immediately recoiled, trying to move away, but his arms tightened slightly and comfortably, and a smile crossed his face.

"It's alright," he whispered. "I'll look after you. I'm here, I'm here. Shh! It's okay."

I relaxed slightly.

I whimpered. "I'm sorry...I'm sorry." I hiccoughed and I looked down at my hands that were clasping and unclasping with my torment. I realized I was apologising to Daz. I couldn't stop even though I knew he wouldn't listen and I would be kicked and hit again while I was down and depressed. I kept saying sorry, until I finally realised I wasn't with Daz, that it was Steve holding me. I didn't know what to do or say. I was so confused. I didn't know what Steve was capable of.

I held my breath, letting it go in a sob, trying hard to keep silent. Steve spoke again.

"Come on, honey. I'll take you home."

He loosened his grip and guided me to his car. When he had settled me in the passenger seat, he slid in to the driver's seat.

"Where should I go?" he asked.

I murmured my address, still feeling so fragile, but questions were rolling around in my mind. I turned to him.

His profile was hard and I knew he was concentrating on his driving.

"How come you were still there?" I asked.

He glanced towards me, going back to concentrating on the road.

"I'd spent too long looking for you to give up when you ran away. I saw Marge, explained my interest in you, and waited for you to finish your shift."

"Oh," I didn't know whether I was pleased that he'd stayed, or unhappy that he hadn't got the message that I didn't want to see him. I knew my response when I had seen him wasn't my true desire – I had been thinking of him with affection for weeks before he had materialized.

It didn't take long before we were at my flat, and he took me to the door. I knew it would be polite to ask him in, but I was still too upset and a little scared to do so.

He didn't hesitate.

"Open the door," he said. "I'll come in and make you a cup of tea. I don't want you to be alone and you need to eat and sleep."

I hesitated.

He could see the panic that still flitted across my face. He carefully and gently took the keys from my cold hands and opened the door. Taking me by my hand he led me to the sofa and helped me to sit down then went into the kitchen. I heard him clatter around, the hiss of the tap filling the kettle and the sound of the water heating. I kept thinking that he shouldn't be here, that I needed to get him out of my flat, but I seemed stuck to the sofa like a limpet on a rock.

A cup of hot tea was placed on the coffee table at my right and Steve sat next to me, taking my hand in his.

"You're frozen," he said, and I laughed weakly, still in a daze.

"I'm not Mimi," I said.

He frowned.

"What?"

I smiled. "Sorry – you obviously aren't up with opera! It's from 'La Bohéme' by Puccini." My voice sounded small and weak as I tried to get my body and mind back to normal. It felt as if the months of trying to heal my self-esteem had crumbled and I was back to the days of staring at the walls of a shabby caravan.

"Really?" he grinned. "Not really my scene. I prefer the Beatles, or the Rolling Stones! And you don't have to say sorry to me." He reached across me and lifted the cup from the table. I flinched, but he didn't comment.

"Here – drink this, and then I'll have to make sure you get comfy and go to bed, and get some sleep."

I put my hands around the cup and felt the warmth seep into my body. We sat quietly for a few moments, then I asked the question that had been niggling at me ever since he had appeared.

"How did you get the black eye?"

Steve didn't answer straight away. I could see he was trying to find the right words. No doubt he was remembering.

***

Steve was back there – talking to Daz. How could he tell her that Daz was such a bastard? He'd told Steve that she was a frigid bitch, and when Steve had become angry, they had started fighting. Daz had ended up with worse injuries than him – although when he'd realised that Steve was willing to fight back, he had folded, into a snivelling wreck, like the bully he was. It was a relief to leave the home that smelled of stale sex and beer. Bottles had been strewn around, and dirty dishes piled high where they had fallen. Ash trays were full, and Daz himself was a mess. Steve couldn't believe that Clare had been here, and he made his disgust known to Daz. He was thankful that Clare had had the sense to leave.

Only a day later, he heard that Daz had become drunk and had picked on another bloke, punching him in a fury, blinded by alcohol, until the young man could no longer stand. The young man had died and Daz had been arrested. He would be in jail for a very long time.

He needed to carefully tell Clare only what she needed to hear.

***

He smiled ruefully.

"I went and saw Daz," he began.

I gasped. I could feel the fear begin again.

Steve rubbed his hands up and down my arms.

"No – don't worry," he said. "I was trying to find out how you were. You must remember I hadn't seen you for ages – it took me a long time to find where you had gone after your marriage."

He stopped and waited until I'd settled again.

"Anyway, he wasn't very co-operative,"

I nodded. I knew what he was like.

"When he took a swing at me and collected," he continued, touching his face with unconscious concern. "I fought back. He was a coward, and told me that you'd gone and he didn't know why!"

I was astounded. He couldn't have been so stupid – surely. He obviously didn't see his behaviour as wrong, and the situation I had found him in with Amy was probably a joke to him. I wondered whether Amy had returned and was with him now. Or had she disappear completely out of the area? Was she now at peace with her mother, and had she given up the life she had been living.

I had no clue. There had been too much self-healing that had to take place for me to worry about Amy or Daz. I had not been in contact with either of them. In fact, I had tried to wipe the horror of my life from my mind, to try and move on, and accept that life wasn't fair. I was still left with anxiety and panic attacks and I wasn't sure if they would ever go. My memories still surfaced every now and again, and I wasn't going to go through that type of life ever again.

Steve continued.

"He was a mess, you know. He was drinking heavily, and he got into another fight. The young man he targeted died from his punches, so he's been arrested and will soon be in jail. He can't hurt you anymore."

I sighed. That was not true. I was still hurt – on the inside. I didn't want to know he was incarcerated – I felt for him – I had loved him to distraction, but his legacy of panic and anxiety attacks, the fear I held deep in my heart, my feelings of unworthiness still rankled. They were hard, if not impossible, to conquer.

Steve sat still, continuing to give me some comfort, but I could feel my eyes beginning to droop. I didn't want to give in. I was still nervous of being alone with him, but Steve must have noticed. He stood up.

"Come on," he said, holding on to both of my hands and pulling me gently from the sofa. "You look beat. I think it's time you went to bed."

I tried to protest. I was terrified once he got me into the bedroom that he would expect sex, get angry with me because my energy had gone and I couldn't respond to him.

He led me to the bed, pulled back the covers, lifted me up and put me on the bed, took off my shoes, pulled the blankets up to my chin and kissed me on the forehead.

"Go to sleep," he counselled with only kindness and concern. "I'll just be in the lounge."

Despite all my misgivings, I think I was asleep before he left the room.

Chapter 13.

I awoke sometime during the night. The flat was dark and silent. I desperately needed two things; the bathroom, and a drink.

I threw back the covers, and discovered I was fully dressed. The memories of yesterday came flooding back.

I sat still, listening. I heard nothing. I concluded that Steve must have gone, so I went out to the bathroom. When I finished, I decided to make myself a hot chocolate. As I walked through the lounge, I nearly shot through the ceiling when I heard a snore. I turned on the light, holding my shaking body ready to attack.

Had Daz found me?

Steve sat up on the couch, his hair and clothes rumpled, his eyes screwed up against the sudden light. He looked half asleep, yet his first words were "Are you okay?"

I breathed again. I didn't want to admit it, but he looked wonderful.

"You're still here?" I swallowed nervously.

Steve blinked several times, ran his fingers through his hair, scowling in the brightness of the light.

"Mmm – of course – I told you I would stay. Damn but this sofa is uncomfortable."

It was three in the morning – but I couldn't help it. My nerves needed release. I began to giggle. I couldn't stop. I had to sit down on the chair opposite him. I was giggling so hard, I was finding it hard to breathe.

"What's so funny?" he glared at me, furrowing his brow at the same time.

How did you tell a man that it was such a relief that he was uncomfortable, in my flat in the middle of the night and not drunk or angry, and that all I wanted was hot chocolate? That I was so relieved that

I had slept without being woken violently. That I was unusually comforted by his mussed hair, cheeky face and ongoing concern. So I forgot my fears, and between gasping and giggling, told him exactly that!

He grinned.

"Better make chocolate for two then," he said.

***

The friendship between Steve and me settled into a comfortable routine. I went to work. He'd pick me up from work. We'd have a coffee and a chat about our day. Sometimes I would cook dinner for us both. Sometimes we went out for dinner. He was a wonderful friend. After dinner, we would part – he off to his place and me to relax and sleep.

I continued to have nights of tears and fear, although I was grateful that they were getting less and less. I always made sure I kept a smiling face for the world, but the events of the last couple of years had left a huge scar on my psyche.

Steve came around on my birthday. He stood at my door, holding a huge bunch of flowers.

I smiled and let him in. He seemed nervous, but I didn't mind. It made him so much more human and loveable.

I went and found a large jar to put the flowers in – I didn't have a vase big enough. When I turned around, he put his arms around me, gave me a quick kiss and began to sing.

"Happy birthday to you, happy birthday to..."

His voice was terrible – I didn't let him finish, flinging myself, laughing, into his arms, sealing his lips with a kiss.

The atmosphere changed immediately. The kiss deepened and his eyes closed as he pulled me close.

My whole body clenched into a ball of tension, as I went back, back to my marriage with Daz. My mind remembered – I must give in. If I didn't, he would hurt me. It would be worse if I resisted.

I forced myself to seem anxious to please, and when he began to caress me, I let it happen.

He dropped the flowers into the vase. The atmosphere was charged with sexual sparks, and he once more enveloped me in his arms. I felt his hands find the skin under my shirt, and he gently moved me towards my bedroom. All the while his lips were on mine. I couldn't think through the haze of fear, but I didn't want to be punched or sworn at if I refused. I felt myself lowered to the bed.

"Oh Clare," he breathed into my neck, as his lips followed the line down towards my breasts. "I've dreamt of this since I first met you."

I cringed inside, willing away the thought that that was a moment I'd tried to forget. I wondered whether the moment of my shame, open to the world, vulnerable, was what had turned him on.

I was now so much more experienced, and I was able to school my body to accept his caresses, and it wasn't long before I was naked, and I was amazed to find I was hot and wet, ready for him. I helped him strip, and we proceeded to dance the old dance of procreation, swaying to the rhythm of lust, the age old method of advancing the human race.

I lost myself in the moment, and when Steve gasped, tensed then slumped over me, I was surprised it was over. I had actually enjoyed the experience, and I wasn't sore or hurting or bruised. I was so shocked, that I burst into tears.

"Oh my God, Clare," Steve pulled me into a warm embrace. "Did I hurt you?"

I couldn't speak. This shouldn't have happened. I didn't know what to say.

I shook my head, tears still running down my face.

"I can't ... I shouldn't ...I ..."

I pushed at him, trying to grab the sheets to cover myself. I was suddenly so embarrassed.

Steve let go and shifted away. He covered me with the bedclothes and got up. I turned my head away, clasping the sheets under my chin. Steve got dressed. He walked out of the bedroom and I sighed with relief holding my bottom lip behind my teeth, trying hard not to cry any more.

I'd almost got my emotions under control, when Steve came back into the room. He put a cup of coffee on the bedside table and sat carefully on the bed.

"I'm so sorry, Clare," he said. "I had no intention of going that far, but I thought you felt the same."

I continued to stare at the wall away from him.

"I love you, Clare." He said. "I always have. Please forgive me."

I swallowed another sob.

"Just go," I sound strangled. "I need you to go."

He placed his hand on my white-knuckled hands, and let the warmth penetrate the ice coldness that I was feeling.

"I'll go," he said. "But I'll be back. I can't leave you like this, and not check that you are going to be all right."

I nodded, but didn't move. I clenched my eyes closed and turned my face away. I felt him stand, and then he was gone.

Chapter 14.

I lay there for ages. Thinking. Crying. Thinking again.

I felt such an idiot. I had painted Steve with Daz's brush. I should have known that he was different, but I had been so frightened. Intimacy was so difficult. What if I wasn't good enough? I realized I loved Steve as I had never loved Daz. It was a warm feeling and an unselfish desire. Yet I worried. Surely he would change. I imagined that he would become disgusted that I had been so soiled by Billy and his gang, as well as the trauma that I had to overcome of the treatment I had received during my marriage. I hadn't told him the extent of the violence and the humiliation and degradation I felt from Daz's actions.

I knew Daz had considered me frigid – a bitch and a failure. He told me often enough. Now Steve was trying to get close, and I couldn't accept that he could love me like he said – I figured it was just in the afterglow of lust and sex. When he discovered the real me, he would change – and even if he didn't get violent – and I couldn't see how he would not – then he would leave me and I would be alone and distraught again.

***

I finally got up, slipped into my dressing gown and, still half asleep, wandered out to make myself a fresh cup of coffee.

I stopped and stared.

Steve was stretched out on the uncomfortable sofa, fast asleep. I didn't know whether to be angry, or happy. I had told him to go, yet he hadn't left.

I crept past to go into the kitchen and turned on the kettle, taking down two coffee cups from my cupboard.

Thoughts kept tumbling around in my head.

Why had he stayed after I had told him to go?

Should I be worried?

Did he really love me?

Could I let down my defences, and let him in to my life?

I was smiling slightly, when arms, snuck around my waist, and Steve whispered into my ear. I immediately tensed, but he spoke softly, held me lightly.

"You look lovely this morning – all rumpled and warm. Are you feeling okay now?"

I turned into his embrace. His lips brushed across my forehead.

I brought my hands up to his chest and pushed him away. I was not sure what to do. My fears were bubbling just under the surface.

"Why are you still here?" I asked my voice husky and tremulous.

Steve smiled, keeping his arms around me and not letting me break the contact.

"I told you I wouldn't leave you alone."

"But ... "

"No buts." He replied, twisting around and grabbing the kettle as it boiled. I stood, suddenly bereft of his warmth. For one dizzying moment I thought he might pour the boiling water on me, but he filled the cups.

"Now that I've seen you're okay, we'll have our cuppa, then I'm off to work." He picked up the teaspoon and stirred the coffee, reaching the fridge, and adding the milk.

I hadn't moved. My face must have registered the sudden panic, but Steve merely picked up the cups and placed them on the table.

He smiled, offered me his hand and helped me to sit on the kitchen chair and then sat opposite me.

It felt somehow right. I actually felt protected and I could see this going into the future, but I didn't want to believe. I was very wary.

We sat comfortably and drank the coffee, with no need for much conversation. I kept looking at Steve, waiting for the explosion. Wondering when he would suddenly erupt into a fury of sex over the kitchen table. I was obviously still looking like a stunned rabbit, caught in the headlights.

"Relax!" he said. "I understand your fears – you haven't exactly experienced a loving relationship."

He placed the empty cup on the bench, came over to me.

I held my breath. Would I be flung onto the table and raped?

He kissed the top of my head, and I heard him breathe in.

"Aah! You smell like cherries!" he remarked, then squatted next to me and cupped my face gently in his hands.

"Be happy." He said. "I'm off to work. I'll see you later."

He stood, squeezed my hand and then walked out.

I let out my breath, relieved that I was alone. I needed to stop my heart beating as if it would jump out of my chest. I needed to stop comparing Steve with Daz. I needed to slow my thoughts, get myself under control and get ready for work. I needed to figure out what I would do next.

I got unsteadily to my feet, went back into the bedroom, stripped off, stood under the shower until I could think rationally again, then got ready for work, walked out the door and started my new day, another hesitant step into my future.

***

Steve carefully wooed me. He didn't make love to me again for a while – he kissed and hugged, but there was no underlying pressure. He seemed to understand I needed more time.

He brought me flowers; he took me out to movies, to dinner, to picnics on the beach. He gradually wore down my terror of intimacy. He held my hand when we walked in the park. He cuddled me when I felt insecure. He cooked for me when I was too exhausted to do it myself. He didn't mention sex, keeping our newfound relationship on a comfortable footing.

Embraces and caresses were gentle and he never pushed me into doing anything I didn't want to do.

A few weeks later, I was expecting him around for the evening and I'd cooked a special meal. I decided that tonight I would love to melt into his arms and make love. We hadn't had sex for weeks, ever since that first time. I was beginning to wonder if I could no longer excite a man, although the act still frightened me, I was willing to try again.

I took great care dressing, with some gorgeous new red panties and matching bra under my slim black cocktail dress that I had splurged on at the shops.

I was happy and relaxed with him, at last.

When there was a knock on the door, I rushed to it, opening it with a huge smile on my face.

I froze.

Daz stood on the doorstep.

"Found you at last – you bitch," he snarled as he pushed past me, yanking me towards the bedroom, as he slammed the door with his foot.

I knew better than to struggle, but I couldn't hide the fear that suffused my whole being.

I didn't make it any further. He turned and slapped me across the face. I felt the warmth of blood trickle from my mouth as I fell on the floor. He followed me down, ripping my dress as he did so.

"Whew!" he exclaimed as my underwear was revealed. "That's more like it – red and sexy, ripe for fucking! That's what I want."

I must have cried out, but the next thing I knew, he was off me, and I was able to scramble away, pushing my feet into the carpet, moving with speed and coiled adrenalin.

Steve had walked in and rescued me – again.

This time, the fight above me was fast and furious. Steve was like a steamroller. I could hear the punches landing on Daz's body with unrelenting anger. Daz began to cower, whimper and sink down with his hands up, asking for mercy.

Steve grabbed the front of his jacket, and pulled him up, bringing his face level with his own.

"If I see you anywhere near here ever again," he growled menacingly into Daz's face, "I can't promise that I'll be so gentle with you next time!" He dragged him to the door and with a mighty shove, threw him out the door.

I had managed to get to my feet, and I saw Daz fall to his knees, get up and run, yelling back over his shoulder something that was so obscene I couldn't believe I had ever found him attractive.

Steve turned and grabbed me, still riding high on adrenalin.

"Are you okay?" he asked, embracing me as if I was made of glass. I nodded, not sure if I really was. He held me close, allowing himself to control the shakes that now beset his body and mine.

"I was so angry," he said into my hair as I found the security and warmth of his chest. "I'm so sorry!"

I looked up at him and frowned.

"You're sorry?" I murmured. "Why?"

He set me back and looked into my eyes.

"I should have been here sooner! I should have stopped him – I should have realized he would come looking for you." He went quiet. "He should be in jail," he muttered. "I'm going to find out what is going on!" He turned rapidly, strode to the phone and rang the police.

Before I could take in the moment, he was back, getting me to sit down, rushing around getting me a cup of tea.

I tried to pull my shredded dress around me to cover my body. Steve dashed into the bedroom and grabbed a blanket.

"Here," he said, placing it around me. I hadn't realised I was shivering with shock.

When the police arrived, Steve took over. I was much stronger this time. I showed the police the scratched, bruises that were already flowering on my body and the ripped dress that I had taken completely off when Steve had settled me with the blanket and tea.

I knew I would be able to put this latest assault behind me, especially when two days later, the police called and told me that Daz was in custody, and would be incarcerated for a long time – there had been extra information surface that had implicated him in the drugs that Amy had taken that had caused her death. He was being charged with murder of the young man he had punched to death as well as drug trafficking and my assault.

I grieved for Amy. I hadn't known what had happened. I wondered if she had ever been reconciled with her mother, and decided that when I got the opportunity I would try and find her and let her know the extent of Amy's trauma and why she had become the person she had.

Steve treated me in the following months with love and never let me dwell on the events that had spun my world once more out of control.

He continued to romance me – making me feel special and cosseted. Sex had still been kept at bay, but never once did I see pity or disgust in his eyes. The sex we had had that once, had been the turning point in our relationship, and I felt ready once again to follow the lead that my heart and body was telling me.

The next time he arrived at my flat with a bouquet of flowers, I was ready. This time, I accepted his kiss with a heat of my own, and we didn't take long to become carried away by passion. My clothes joined his on the floor as we moved, without losing contact, mouth to mouth, hands touching bare skin.

My skin felt flushed and aching with need.

He stretched, naked and aroused, next to me just looking.

I wanted to cover myself, and went to pull the sheet up over my body.

He held my hand.

"Don't." He pleaded. "Let me look." His eyes travelled after his fingers, up and down from neck to breast, stopping to caress, then cover each nipple with a hot and sexy mouth. He continued down my body, until I arched up to meet his fingers, then mouth, calling out his name as I was pushed over the brink.

He lifted his head and looked at me. I'm sure my eyes were glazed with pleasure.

"You're beautiful," he sighed, moving up to my lips, entering me as he kissed me.

I didn't think I could cope any more, but I came again and again, until with a cry and a gasp we both hit a new high, rolling into heaven on a wave of supreme pleasure.

***

Once the gates had opened, we spent every night in bed. I had never imagined sex could be so wonderful. Fear of being hurt disappeared. Steve was so gentle, so loving, that even when we were so anxious for one another that the sex was hot, strong and quick, there was never any thought of violence.

When he asked me to marry him, it felt right. I didn't hesitate. I was over the moon – and, I suspected, pregnant as well. When I told Steve my thoughts, he was thrilled.

"Yay!" he shouted, lifting me into the air with his exuberance. "That's fabulous."

I was astonished that he wasn't in the least bit worried or angry with me. I knew there was going to be times in my life that the fear would surface every now and again, but it was getting less and less often.

I rang Betty and Tony, bubbling over with happiness. After she had called Tony over to the phone and they had congratulated me, she stopped and said, very quietly,

"When are you going to let your parents know?"

I hadn't spoken to my parents since they had blamed me for the failure of my marriage to Daz.

What was I going to do?

I swallowed.

"I'll ask Steve what he thinks," I answered.

"I think they deserve to know." Betty said.

When I spoke to Steve later, he agreed with Betty.

"They deserve to know," he said, echoing Betty's words. "Surely they will be happy for their only daughter? And they will be having grandchildren." He laughed. "We're not going to stop at one, you know!"

"But what if I lose it? I hadn't been able to stay pregnant when I was with Daz. Why would I keep this baby?"

"My darling – I'll love and spoil you so much that the baby will be fine. After all the stress and fear you experienced before it's not surprising your body gave up and you couldn't keep the babies. It isn't going to happen this time. I'm going to wrap you in cotton wool, my love. You and the little one will be fine. Absolutely fine!!"

It took all the courage I could conjure, but I rang my parents the next day, and invited them to our wedding in the future. The reaction was extreme.

"We will not recognize the marriage," Mum said before she cut me off by putting the phone down firmly. I hadn't told her where we were, or when the wedding would be held. She obviously didn't want to know. I could see her face in my mind's eye – compressed lips, hard eyes – no compassion at all.

I decided then and there to forget them. From now on Betty and Tony were my parents.

Epilogue.

It took only six weeks for my divorce from Daz to go through. The circumstances were exceptional and the magistrate compassionate. We had already been separated for the necessary length of time, and, with Daz in jail, it was a foregone conclusion.

Steve and I got married the very next day, in the little church just down the road. The church service was brief, but Betty and Tony stood up proudly for me. Several of the staff from work made the effort to come, and I was pleasantly surprised that so many had considered me a friend.

Many of Steve's friends and family turned up, smiling and happy for him.

"Clare, my love," his sister gushed. "You look positively radiant."

I blushed. We had told no-one that I was pregnant, so she wasn't aware of the fact. I wasn't in white, as I felt that I was not, nor had I been for a long time, 'pure' as dressing in white suggests. They all knew I had been married before but the details hadn't been broadcast.

My dress of apricot swirled around my legs, as Steve held my hand and beamed at his elder sister.

"She does, doesn't she?" he said, looking at me with adoration.

I lowered my eyes. I still couldn't believe anyone, let alone a handsome man like Steve, could love me so completely.

After the wedding, we bought a lovely little house in the suburbs. I couldn't contain my excitement. We would have a garden, and Tony had already offered his help to landscape the yard.

Betty visited and hugged me as we looked at the spare room.

"Can you just see this room?" she bubbled. "Such a lovely room for a nursery."

I grinned.

"I'm way ahead of you," I giggled, loving seeing her so happy and in her element.

"Would you do a kid's mural on the wall?" I asked.

"Of course!!" She was ecstatic.

And so our life together began.

It wasn't long before we were cuddling our son, and then, some two years later, our daughter.

Every now and again, my demons would surface, but Steve understood and calmed my fears. Each episode got less and less frightening and further and further apart.

I couldn't have been happier.

Maureen Larter writes in several genres, from adult urban drama to toddlers picture books. (When writing for adults, she does so under the name **Marguerite Wellbourne**). She lives on the North Coast of New South Wales in Australia. All her books are set in Australia.

She lives on a small-holding of 15 acres and endeavors to be as self-sufficient as possible, with a large vegetable garden and orchard, several chickens for eggs, and bees for honey.

If she isn't outside looking after animals or gardens, she is on the computer - writing .

www.ingramcontent.com/pod-product-compliance
Lightning Source LLC
Chambersburg PA
CBHW051951290426
44110CB00015B/2200